# RISING ABOVE

## A MEMOIR ABOUT FAMILY BETRAYAL, AND GROWING INTO FORGIVENESS

## BRUNO DELUCA

authorHOUSE°

*AuthorHouse™*
*1663 Liberty Drive*
*Bloomington, IN 47403*
*www.authorhouse.com*
*Phone: 1 (800) 839-8640*

*Published by AuthorHouse   01/26/2017*

*ISBN: 978-1-5246-5963-9 (sc)*
*ISBN: 978-1-5246-5964-6 (hc)*
*ISBN: 978-1-5246-5962-2 (e)*

*Library of Congress Control Number: 2017900531*

*Print information available on the last page.*

*Any people depicted in stock imagery provided by Thinkstock are models, and such images are being used for illustrative purposes only. Certain stock imagery © Thinkstock.*

*This book is printed on acid-free paper.*

*This book is dedicated to my kids. It is my hope that it will help you in the future with your friends and family.*

*Children, obey your parents in the Lord, for this is right. "Honor your father and mother"—this is the first commandment with a promise: "so that it may be well with you and you may live long on the earth." And, fathers, do not provoke your children to anger, but bring them up in the discipline and instruction of the Lord.*

*Ephesians 6:1-4*

My father, Giovanni, was born in Calabria, Italy, in 1943. He was the youngest of three sisters and three brothers. The family was very poor. The family safe contained their most valuable item: bread! It had to be rationed properly so that all the kids had their fair share. I remember Dad telling me the story that when he was eating the bread he would pretend that he was eating a cheese sandwich.

My Uncle Sandro, the eldest of the seven kids, once told me that they all thought that young Johnny was special and different from the rest of them. He was restless and not happy simply accepting his lot in life.

At twelve, my dad already had a businessman's mind. Somehow, he was able to convince a shopkeeper to loan him a case of pop. He said that he would bring the money later, plus extra for the trouble. He took the pop and sold it by the can to certain "businessmen" that sat around playing cards all day in the town square.

As promised, he brought back the money to the shopkeeper, plus extra, and a little for himself too. After that, the shopkeeper trusted him and was willing to let him come for the pop whenever he needed it.

At the age of sixteen, Dad decided to immigrate to the United States of America to find a better life. He had family in New York willing to help him out. Unfortunately, it didn't work out so well. He was working as a driver delivering to bakeries around the city. He parked the van somewhere he was not supposed to, but he didn't know the city very well or where else to go to make his delivery. There was a cop waiting for him when he got out. The details are vague, and my dad never really told us the whole tale. The most he ever said to anyone was to my wife.

"I could tell by his eyes that he was going to hurt me," he told her. "Maybe even kill me."

I can believe it. Remember, this was the late 1950s. These were difficult years in the States for racial unrest. I can imagine that the cop had negative feelings toward Italians, or my dad was trespassing on some kind of gang territory, and this cop was on the take. Either way, my dad went with his gut, grabbed a handy piece of wood, and beat the cop. How badly? Who knows? He was arrested and charged. My dad obviously had some connections in New York. He was able to get out on bail, and his friends got him north of the border quickly. He has not set foot in the United States since, so there is definitely some truth to this story.

In this day and age, it is hard to understand the kind of racism that existed then. My parents weren't innocent either. When I started dating, my mother told me never to bring a *nigger* home. Apparently there is already black in my family and it is a big secret. Nobody likes to talk about it. Ridiculous! I just don't understand it at all.

I did date a beautiful black woman for two years. Alisha was very sweet. She was divorced and had two boys who loved the Italian national soccer team. It was nice being with her and experiencing the Somalian culture. Likewise, I would cook Italian dishes for her. I liked her and the boys very much, but it was not meant to be. I was not in love. It had nothing to do with our races. If I had truly loved her I wouldn't have cared what my family thought. Even she said that her family would have an issue with me being white.

Look how great our lives are for having all sorts of different cultures in our country. Where would the sushi restaurants be, the Caribbean festivals, and all other kinds of art and knowledge without people mingling races? At the end of the day, God only recognizes one race—the human race. As individuals we are all valuable and precious in God's sight.

In Canada, my dad started working in construction. He worked odd jobs as a laborer and a painter. What he really wanted, though, was to learn how to make desserts. Back in the day, he had no money to go to school, and nobody was willing to teach him. Trade secrets were guarded carefully. The only way he could learn about recipes and baking was to watch and remember.

He took a job at Gianni's Bakery as a driver. Between deliveries he watched and learned, sneaking off to the bathroom to write down what he saw. Once he felt he had something to work with, he moved on to his next job at Cakes & Sweets Bakery. The owner took an interest in him and was willing to teach him how to make cookies, pastries, and cakes. His colleagues there used to call him *il ratto,* "the rat," because he was so fast.

He also worked at Cakes-To-Go, and all he did was cakes. He said it was a nice experience because he learned so much even though he was only there for a short time.

My dad met Maria, my mother, through a family member. My mom came from the complete opposite walk of life from my father. She was the oldest child from a rich family, with a father that she admittedly says spoiled her rotten.

"Whatever I want, I got," she said.

I don't know how my father charmed her, but they were married in 1964.

I was born in May of 1966—what day in May depends on who you ask. My mother says May 20, my birth certificate says May 21, and my health insurance says May 22. I have no idea how this happened. I suspect my mother's lack of English skills may have played a part.

My mom said she had a hard time carrying me. Her doctor must have been a complete idiot. She complained of swelling and was told that all pregnant women have swelling. My mom delivered me in a severe state of toxemia. I was underweight, but apparently I made up for it as soon as I could and turned into a chubby baby. One day when my mom left me in my dad's care, he fed me *nine* jars of baby food in one go.

"Well, he was hungry!" he said when my mother found out.

Dad couldn't have been happier to have a son. He wanted to name me after his brother, Bruno, who was not able to have his own children. I heard stories that he would rush home after work just to see me, and that as soon as I was able to walk, I would come running to the window as I heard his car pulling in. Growing up, I loved my father very much.

My parents say that as a baby and a young boy I always wanted things my own way. For example, there was a time when my mother made spaghetti and I did not want it, so I hid it in the plants. My mother lost her shit. You just do not do that in an Italian home! Then she spanked me and I got so upset that I ran around the table knocking all the chairs down. She spanked me again and then I ran under the kitchen table and turned it completely over. All this time my dad was laughing.

My mom shouted, "Why are you laughing?"

"This kid doesn't understand when you spank him, the more you hit him the worse he is."

My father said this is the kind of person he is too—he wants things his way. That is funny because even today this is true.

My brother Rocco came along in 1968. Here is another weird tale that no one really talks about much: all he did was cry, nonstop. Now, I know all babies cry, my mother had her fair share of crying babies as an older sister, plus she'd already had me. But Rocco, apparently, *never stopped* crying.

"If he was awake, he was crying," my mom said.

So, my mother took him to the same idiot doctor who told her not to worry about severe swelling, and he of course brushed her off.

After a while my mom just could not take it anymore. She had a nervous breakdown and had to be hospitalized for six months! I'm sure postpartum depression had something to do with this, but remember that this was the 1960s we're talking about. My Zia Angela took care of us during that time.

I can't help but think that something was seriously wrong with my brother when he was a baby. I wonder if things would have worked out differently if the doctor had cared more. To this day Rocco has what I guess you would call learning disabilities. He is still not able to read very well, although he is a genius with other things.

My parents didn't care. Basically they told the schools that Rocco was their problem. I wonder what would have happened if he had gotten the help he needed. He could have been the Wolf of Wall Street.

At the time that Rocco was born, my dad had made a leap and opened up his own bakery—Pisa Bakery—in Toronto. He did pizza along with his pastries and actually became best known for his pizza. He owned that bakery for three years and then his father-in-law asked him to come back to Italy and start a business with him there. So with a wife and two little boys in tow, my dad packed up and went back to the mother country.

I have to give my dad credit, selling off all his accomplishments just to go back to Italy. He didn't really want to go, but my mom did. I don't think she was ever happy here in Canada. Dad must have loved her very much to do that for her.

Unfortunately, my grandfather reneged on the whole business venture. I think the real reason he asked my dad to go into business with him was to get his daughter and grandsons close to him. About half a year later it became clear that there would be no business. My dad packed up again and we were going back to Canada. My mother was upset, as all her family was still in Italy at the time. In those days, a woman did what she was told to do by her husband. In this case though, I believe my dad was in the right. The opportunities were far better in Canada for him and the whole family.

Back in Canada, Dad started work in a bakery called Tom's Italian bakery. The owner decided to sell the business, and my dad jumped on the opportunity. He bought the store and the unit beside it, and changed the name to La Lucca bakery.

When you're a little kid, everything is always seems good. My dad was my hero and I truly believed I was number one in his life. All I wanted was to be as great as my dad.

My parents put me in hockey for two years and that was a lot of fun. Dad also made sure my brother and I played soccer. I loved soccer. I played for five years. I have four trophies from soccer and two from ice hockey. If it was a sport, I was into it. I was captain of the volleyball and hockey team in grade school. I was also very good at track and field.

When I was around nine years of age my mother told me I had be careful whenever I went out. All parents tell their kids not to talk to strangers. My mom was no different than any other mother. This day though, something was up. She was extra nervous, and seemed reluctant to let me out on my own at all.

"Watch out all around you. If someone is following you don't let them get too close," she said. "You run back home as fast as you can!"

"I never talk to strangers, Mama!" I said. "Why are you so worried?"

"You just watch yourself!" she replied. "You don't let anyone take you! *Capito?*"

"I understand, Mama."

I didn't know what was going on during that period of time, but whatever it was, the way my mother was acting scared me to death. I still don't know what was up, but I think my father was involved with some bad people. I'm guessing something had gone wrong and his family may have been targets for some kind of revenge. This is something that is very hard to get my dad to talk about, so I guess I will never know.

Can you imagine walking to school under that kind of stress? I must have looked like I was scared because I started to get picked on. It got worse when I went into junior high school; I kept getting beat up. My father's solution was to put me in martial arts. Like most boys in the 70's I was a Bruce Lee fan, so Kung-Fu and kick boxing it was for me.

One day the school bully approached me and started causing trouble. He pushed me around, wanting to start a fight.

"I hear you take Kung-Fu," he said, giving my shoulder a shove. You think you're tough?" He gave me another shove.

"It's not about being tough," I told him. "Why do you want to fight me? I did nothing to you."

"What's wrong? You chicken?" He shoved me again.

"If you want a fight, we can fight, but you will lose."

He laughed!

"Make your move," I shrugged.

I dodged his first punch, and as he flailed at me again, I grabbed him in a hold and dropped him. Then it was my turn for punching! I hurt him very badly and he never bothered me again. I don't think he ever bothered *anyone* after that!

I wasn't proud of what I did. Besides being in Kung-Fu, I had joined the Cadets. These things taught me respect for others and discipline. Maybe I should have walked away from it, but what would have happened? He might've stopped bothering me, but he probably would have picked on someone else instead. I hope that encounter made him think twice about his behavior.

When I wasn't beating up the neighborhood bully, I was playing street hockey. This is a physical sport, but you have to play with your mind too. I was really good at it and I had a lot of fun. I played whenever I had a chance since Dad had me working with him by the time I was eleven. I used to work a lot. That took most of my play time away.

In High school I bought my own drum set and took lessons. My buddy played bass, and like most high school kids, we had dreams of forming a band. I would have liked to have continued but as I was working more and more, I had less and less time for extra-curricular activities and my friends.

When I turned sixteen, my father bought me a KD 80 Kawasaki dirt bike. It was a nice bike! After a year of burning rubber with it I decided to get myself an even bigger one. The reason I wanted a new one so badly was a girl named Elaine that I wanted to impress. I saved my money and purchased a Suzuki 125 and it was a beauty! Well, Elaine became my girlfriend, and she loved the bike as much as I did. It was a great time and I had a lot fun.

My relationship with Elaine wasn't easy because I worked so much. We did have lots of good times whenever we were able to be together.

Her dad did not like me because I had long hair and that did not sit well with him, but it did not stop her from being my girlfriend. One night I was at her house watching a movie. We stepped outside and we started making out. I saw her dad watching us through the window. I thought he was going to kill me, but he had a wry smile on his face. I broke away from Elaine gently and told her.

"That's my dad," she laughed.

That is a father watching out for his daughter and I respect that. As time went by I listened to my friends and let her go. It was stupid of me because I had very strong feelings for her at the time. If I were to ever see her again I would thank her. She cared about me when I was going through a tough time.

My dad wanted me to quit school and work full-time but I didn't want that. I graduated from high school and then started work. Later I would go into business with my Dad and that would change my whole life.

I was always a very religious person. This I owe to my mother. Like most Italians we were Catholic. When I was ten, I had a dream of the Virgin Mary. She told me my mother was pregnant with a baby girl. Sure enough, about a month later my mother told me that she was pregnant.

I said, "I know! You are going to have a girl." Then I told her about the dream.

Nina came into the world that October. My mother believed that I was blessed and destined to become a priest. I never thought about being a priest at that age, but it wasn't my calling anyway. Still, I have always felt the hand of God in my life.

Sometimes when I think about my father, I remember how much he loved music. I guess that's where I got it from. My sister used to sing, and my dad brought her to a music teacher when she was nine to see if she had what it took to be a great singer. He heard her once, and told my dad she was very gifted. So my dad decided to write an album.

He hired a popular Italian singer and had a special song in there just for my sister. It became very well-known in Italian circles. Nina began to sing in public for events, and even performed at Canada's Wonderland for the CHIN International festival.

At the same time, the business that my brother and I opened with our dad was growing and becoming a brand name among the Italian community and beyond. Everyone knew who we were and who Nina was. I think it was embarrassing for her.

When Nina was fifteen, she decided she didn't want to do Italian music anymore. I remember Dad trying to explain to her that he only had connections in the Italian music industry. If she got very famous in Italy then it would be easier for her to move into the English part of the industry.

She insisted that she would not do any more Italian music because her friends were making fun of her. Everyone tried to tell her how foolish she was being, but she had her mind made up. I guess she was as stubborn as her big brother!

After she got married, she brought it up to me how much she regretted that decision. By then it was too late. I truly believe that paths open up for you, but you must take them to see where they lead you. You can't let the jealousy and remarks of hurtful people stand in your way. I think my sister still cares too much what other people think.

*In all toil there is profit, but mere talk tends only to want.*

*Proverbs 14:23-24*

My father did very well with La Lucca Bakery. He used to go through 240 bags of flour a week. Also a couple hundred cakes, and all kinds of pastries. You may be reading this and wondering if that is good. Well, in retail that is *very* good, where most bakeries might do 50 to 80 bags of flour a week and a minimum of cakes and pastries. He also thought it would be a good idea to make his own gelato.

I loved my dad's gelato! It was amazing! So many different flavors, but my favorite was chocolate and banana. I had a sweet tooth and loved his cannoli and the Neapolitan pastries too.

When I was eleven I helped the bakers and pastry chefs with whatever they needed. As I got older and started getting better at the job, I was in every morning and weekend. I loved that bakery, but I also hated it for taking so much of my youth away.

Sometimes it was so hard on me that I would fall asleep during class. For my father, work was more important than school. He never had an education, so he didn't think his sons needed one either. While I really don't appreciate Dad's attitude towards higher education, I have to admire his work ethic. He passed that on to me and Rocco at an early age.

The business did well, but my dad's health was not good. As time went by, it came to a point where he could not even move. My mother decided to bring in a spiritual woman who had the gift of laying on of hands. For those not familiar with that term, it means that she would touch someone, pray over them and they would be healed.

After many hours of praying over my dad, he was able to get up and walk. It was truly a miracle!

Once he was able to walk again, Dad took my mother's advice and put the bakery up for sale. Within a few months the bakery was sold. He took some time off and enjoyed it. We went to Italy for a family vacation and stayed for two months.

Unfortunately, my grandfather had become very ill with cancer. During our vacation we made sure we spent some time with him. I was Nonno's favorite grandchild, but that was only between us. He was so good to me, he would always give me money and tell me not to tell my parents. It was always our secret. I loved him so much. When he had his health, he was a very tall and strong man. This is where I got my height from. My father is a very short man!

In the hospital room next to my nonno there was a mobster. The newspapers said he got shot eighteen times and it didn't kill him! I peeked into the room to see two police officers there guarding him. I also remember looking into his wife eyes. She looked like she had a hard life. I was sad to see her in that position, I don't think she ever thought she'd end up in life like that.

My nonno was very agitated being in the room next to him. The mob used to go by his store for money every month. I remember my nonna always upset because she had to give it to these people. If they hadn't they would probably have blown up the store. Yes, this happens for real, not just in the movies! My uncle had refused to pay and his store was destroyed! Can you imagine that happening to your family? What do you do?

Life is very hard for the Italian people that are good and honest. My grandparents chose to live the honest life and pass that on to their children. That is why I feel sad for that woman in the hospital. She chose that life, and it is a life of misery. Some people think being in the mob is glamorous; it isn't! They can never have any peace, never relax and be at ease. I actually said a pray for her, may God help her.

We went to see Nonno for the last time before we went back to Canada. During those few days he would not let anyone else near him, only me. I said my good-byes, but my heart was in so much pain.

I knew that my nonno did not want to die. I told him that I loved him so much and he would be get better.

A month after we came home, Nonno passed away. We were all very saddened by the loss. I could not stop crying because I loved him so much. He may have lied to my dad all those years ago but all in all he was a good man.

*...Because the Lord was a witness between you and the wife of your youth, to whom you have been faithless, though she is your companion and your wife by covenant. Did not the one God make her? Both flesh and spirit are His ... So look to yourselves, and do not let anyone be faithless to the wife of his youth.*

*Malachi 2:14, 15*

It was my last year of High School and all was good with me. We were out of the business and I felt I had my life back. Unfortunately, my parents were not happy. Every day I could hear them fighting.

My dad blamed Mom for making him sell the business. He wanted to do something more with his life. My mother didn't understand why he couldn't just work part time for someone, because we would have been fine. The house was paid and he had money in the bank. That did not mean anything to Dad, he just wanted to be back in business.

Time went by and later in the year my dad makes this big announcement to the whole family. He told us he was leaving to be with another woman.

My mother was devastated when she heard this. I could not believe it, it broke my heart. My brother was also very upset. At the time Nina was only about five years old, we have never really talked about it so I don't know what she remembers or how she felt about it.

My father had even bought a house for this woman in secret! He wanted to start up a clothing business with her. As for us kids, he would grace us with his presence every two weeks.

I can remember lying in bed and hearing my mother crying in the middle of the night. My heart was broken; for me and for her.

Everything she had ever done in life she had done for my father. She must have felt like her life was over.

Life went on, but it was hard. My brother and I weren't little kids anymore, but it was still hard to understand why this was happening. It might have been easier if Dad had have just left her for good, but for the next two years he had this on-again-off-again relationship with the other woman. When it wasn't working out as fine as he wanted he came begging back to my mother. She would always forgive him and take him back! This happened at least seven times!

At some point during those years Rocco had gone to live with Dad. He said he felt bad for him being without his kids. My brother has always been easily manipulated by my father. He tried to talk me into coming with him too, but I would never abandon my mother.

Can you imagine this happening to you? What would you do if you were my mother? How would you feel if you were me, or Nina? My mom tried to go on with her life. She went out with friends to dance clubs, but after a while she stopped going. I guess she really did love my father and didn't want anyone else in her life. Guilt probably played a big part too. She was very religious and traditional. You're just *not* supposed to get divorced! It wasn't fair to her because she was trying to make it work and my dad just kept leaving.

One night Dad came over to see me and my sister. He showed us photographs, supposedly of my mom naked with another man. There was no photo shop back then. He must have known someone who could doctor those photos. I knew they couldn't be real. There was *no possible way* my mom could ever cheat on my dad. She was way too religious. I couldn't believe that my dad could do something so evil, just to get his own way. My sister was so angry she kicked him in the leg. He tried to grab her but she hid behind me. I told him to get out.

The next time I saw Rocco, I told him to tell Dad that I would kill him if he ever hurt my mother. Later my brother told me that I had made Dad so angry that he was threatening to kill me.

"Let him try!" I said. I was so angry, I hated him so much.

I'm sure I wasn't the only teenage boy in a situation like this. It wasn't my fault, but at the time I blamed myself. I started doing drugs, thinking that my problems would go away. I was not eating well and later in life it would catch up with me. I would ask God, why me? Why our family? I just could not understand at that age.

After two years the other woman had enough of my dad or he was finally done with her. Either way, he came crawling back to Mom again looking for forgiveness. My mother didn't take him back right away. She wanted to discuss it with me first.

"What do you think I should do?"

"Tell him to take a hike," I said. "I can quit school and get a job. I'll take care of you and Nina."

I could see in her eyes that this was not what she had wanted to hear. She knew I was right, but she couldn't bring herself to do it.

"In the end it is your decision," I told her.

She took him back, and this time he stayed for good.

It was very uncomfortable around the house for a long time when my father came back. He was trying to act like a real father, but I saw him in a completely different way. My hero was destroyed in my eyes. I couldn't forgive him for what he had put us all through. I had seen his true self, the one that always put his own interests before his family.

I asked my mom if he had always been that way. She says no. He always used to be kind and compassionate to us. I think going into business must have changed him. You've heard the saying that money is the root of all evil and in this case I think it is absolutely true. He was so poor when he was young. Once he had all this money, he felt he could do as he pleased. It seemed like he felt that he could treat his family any way he liked as if he had the right to do it because he made all the money.

When you marry someone, you are supposed to love them. Whatever you do should be done to support each other and the whole family. To be the leader or father of a family does not mean you are entitled to getting your own way. A *true* leader puts his people first. There is nothing wrong with having money, but you should not let it control you. When you let money change you and you put the *money* first, this where it all goes wrong.

All this marital unrest gave me a poor view of marriage. I had no interest in getting married, especially after what I had seen happen with my parents.

*What do mortals get from all the toil and strain with which they toil under the sun? For all their days are full of pain, and their work is a vexation; even at night their minds do not rest. This also is vanity.*

*Ecclesiastes 2:22-24*

M y father was determined to get back into the bakery business. My mother did not want him to go into business again because she worried about his health. Also, she was so afraid of him leaving her again. She thought that if Rocco and I were partners with him, it might keep him at home more and also make him happy. She approached us and asked if we would do it. We said that we would, and waited for Dad to approach us and ask. We pretended as if we did not know it was coming, so he would think it was his idea. To this day he still doesn't know it was Mom that asked us first.

I did try to delay it for as long as I could, since I really didn't want to do it. I told my father that what I truly wanted was to go to college. I've already mentioned my dad's opinion on getting a higher education, so that argument fell on deaf ears.

I was working part-time at Miracle Food Mart. Rocco was working in store called the Farm Market. In the eighties, the pay in the grocery stores was very good. My father had raised us with a very strict work ethic and it served both my brother and I well in our jobs.

I may not have any papers to prove my education in the bakery business, but the lead baker there was impressed with my skills. He was a licensed baker and he asked where I had gone to college. When I told him I hadn't gone anywhere, he was very surprised. He was going to be retiring soon; he and the store manager wanted me to replace him. That meant a lot to me, hearing that from a licensed baker. Just before we went into business, I had been offered the full time job. I would have been well-off if I had stayed there.

My brother was only seventeen at the time. He had never done very well at school. Quitting to work full time was not a tough decision for him and my dad had encouraged it. The funny thing is even as a kid Rocco had a gift for making money. If my parents were more supportive of his education, who knows what accomplishments he could have made. I joke now with my wife, that guy could have been the CEO of a huge corporation. His colleagues and investors would have loved him because all he is about is making money. He had done very well at the farm market. He was already the Lead Baker! He must have been the youngest Lead Baker in the country. His manager hadn't want to lose him either.

In 1985 my father, brother and I went into business for ourselves. It was the start of something great and something that completely changed the course of my life. I was only nineteen years old! I had hoped to go to study business or be a sound engineer. I knew going into business would put an end to those plans. There would be no money and time for anything else.

We bought a bakery in Mississauga called La Roma for $70,000. The business was very run down and the owner knew he wasn't going anywhere with it as it was. We completely gutted the place. When the renovations were done the store was double its original size. We hired an artist to do four murals of different famous spots in Italy; Naples, Florence, Venice and Rome. It was beautiful!

So there Rocco and I were, with very little knowledge of how to run a business and trusting Dad to lead us. We were ready to rock and roll.

The first two weeks my father was going crazy making himself sick with worry. Things were not picking up as fast as he hoped. He was afraid that we wouldn't make enough money to cover the rent. I tried to get him to calm down. We had only just started! What I really think was bothering him was that he had to work so much in the beginning. He had hoped it would just be successful from the get go. I suppose he felt his reputation was enough to get it going. You have to understand that back then, the Italian community really stuck together. We looked after our own and supported each other's businesses, but there are more than just Italian people out in the world!

In my opinion the business was starting out just fine. We were making money. Our rent was $2700 a month for 3500sq ft. We were making $30,000 a month! I'm pretty sure that covered all our expenses. It might have been tight, but we were still new. This wasn't enough for my dad though. I truly believed he was telling me the truth when he said were weren't making any money. After all, why would he lie to us?

After three years the bakery was making $30,000 a week, which is $1.5 million a year. Today that is the equivalent of $3.2 million a year. I hope that makes it easier to understand the money that was there at the time and why my brother and I would be so angry later on.

Looking back, I don't think that my dad ever wanted me to be a good pastry chef. I know that doesn't make any sense! I had to be good to make our business successful after all. That is what it felt like though. Maybe he was threatened by me. He always had to be the best.

He always used to say: "You are good, but I'm better."

I just don't understand that. Doesn't everyone want their kids to do well? If you are teaching your child a skill and one day they surpass you, isn't that a credit to you as a teacher? Why wouldn't you be proud of that?

Many years later, sitting around a campfire with my wife and her parents, we were listening to the neighboring camper play the guitar and sing. We clapped after, and the young lady's father proudly announced:

"I taught her everything she knows. I'm good, but she's better!"

He sounded so proud of her, and I felt a pain in my heart, wishing that I had a father like that.

My wife has helped me so much over the years. I always wondered what was wrong with me as a son. She has made me come to see that my father was insecure. That was why he always had to be the best and to put me down. It is just the kind of man that he is. Maybe so, but why? If it was because of his upbringing, then *what* happened? I would love to ask him about his life with his father, but he won't be honest. There is nothing that I could ever do to change him, but I can change me. My attitude is that there are many great pastry chefs out there, and no matter how good you are, you can always learn something new from somebody.

When I was young it was really hard. I was still learning, and I truly wanted to make my dad proud of me. Every time he taught me something, if I didn't get it exactly right the first time he would humiliate me.

"Even an idiot could do better!"

Or:

"Why are you so stupid?"

You get the idea.

"How can you be a great chef if you can't get it right the first time?!" he scolded me.

"I'm not you, Dad!" I yelled back. "We're not all the same!"

According to him, he never made any mistakes and he learned everything the first time he tried. I highly doubt that now, but when I was only a teenager, I just took for granted that what he said was true.

Sometimes, I fought back. I remember us arguing quite often. I didn't give up though. I tried harder. I believed that eventually, he would acknowledge my skill.

It never happened though. It didn't matter what it was, cakes, cookies, pastries. He never gave me one word of praise. I will never forget the day I made some beautiful cakes with new decoration I had never done before.

"I suppose they're okay," my dad said as I was putting them in the display.

After my father had walked away, one of our bakers approached me.

"Never mind what your dad says," Sal said. "Those cakes are beautiful. You are very talented."

"Thank you, Sal. That means a lot to me!"

I remember how good it felt to hear him say that. I was almost moved to tears. It wasn't my father saying it, but it was finally *proof* to me that I was good! Other people could see it! My staff and my customers made me see the truth.

I don't mean to sound ungrateful. I appreciate everything that my dad taught me. I thought my father was great at what he did. I am as good as I am today *because* of him. I'm happy that he wanted to teach me, but at the same time, I get the feeling that he didn't want to teach me *too much*. There were days that I felt so alone, but I had passion for the work and when you have that passion, you can take a lot of crap.

One day, Rocco made a mistake with the Sicilian bread and buns so that after they were baked, they looked old. It didn't matter to him, he put it out anyway. My dad brought it all back into the kitchen.

"What is this?" he asked my brother.

Rocco replied, "I made a mistake."

Dad said, "That's fine, but you don't put it out in the store to sell."

"Why not? It only happened once."

"Once is enough! If it is not perfect, you don't put it out there! It only takes once to ruin your reputation."

I thank my dad for giving us this work ethic. He set the standards high, and we still live by them today. Those type of lessons were good ones, but most my father's ideology was not very positive. For example, everything in life comes hard, life is not about fun, your dreams don't come true, and never trust anyone. The most positive thing he had to teach was that you should always work for yourself and that was it! I think it's sad, to tell the truth.

I always wanted to have fun in the business because life is too short just to think about money. Just because you are working hard, doesn't mean that you can't enjoy yourself along the way. As long as you are working hard to chase your dream, then how can you not be successful?

If you have a dream, follow your heart. Make sure you understand what needs to be done before you leap into your adventure. Remember we all make mistakes during that journey, but when you come to that, you take it as a lesson, learn from it and move on. People who are successful, are people who have already made their mistakes. Also, people who are successful don't just sit back on their laurels and enjoy the glory. They look to people who are more successful than they are and learn from them.

Now, my father taught us another lesson too. The customer is *not* always right. Yes, you read that right! Everyone has stories about *those* kinds of customers, the ones that you can't please no matter what; the ones that come in just to complain and cause trouble just because they can. And of course the ones that are always trying a *scam*. You can't tolerate those kind of people in a small business. It's not worth it to deal with them. Big chain stores can absorb the loss in other ways so they might cater to that nonsense. When we had a strong reputation like we did at La Roma, we weren't too worried about those kind of people.

Case in point, one day Dad did this beautiful cake for a baby shower. It was very big, what we call a full slab in the business. The trim was pink and blue and it was decorated with roses and confetti. When the lady and her daughter came in to pick it up, she turned up her nose at it!

"That's not what I wanted!" she exclaimed, "I asked for only two colors, not three!" (I guess she didn't like green leaves on the roses?)

"I've taken cake decorating courses, and I could do a better job than that!" the daughter sniffed.

"So why didn't you do it then?" my dad fired back. The daughter turned red and didn't say anything.

"Okay," my dad said to the mother. "Come on over here and show me what I can do to fix this cake."

That wasn't what she wanted to hear of course, no doubt what she wanted was a big discount, or a free cake. Dad sat down and lit up a cigarette. (Yes, you could still do that back then!) The customer went over and started to tell him what she wanted changed. I guess my dad's calm demeanor had her ruffled.

"Oh never mind," she said. "I guess I just have to take it as it is!"

"No, wait!" said my dad. "I do see a mistake here. Let me fix it."

What happened next, I will never forget! He picks up a *huge* cake knife. The big serrated ones we used for cutting the full slabs. Then he just *lays* into the cake! Chopping away, chunks of cake flying everywhere! I wish I had known what he was going to do, I would have taken pictures. We didn't have cell phones then to snap instant videos! Once he was done, there was dead silence. Everyone was in total shock, especially the two who needed the cake.

"Now get the fuck out of my store!" my dad yelled.

Those two ladies literally *ran* out of the store. Believe or not, everyone else in the store including the other customers were clapping and laughing. But you know what? Six months later the *stronza* comes back for another cake. No drama, this time though!

It really bothers me when people say they took a cake decorating course and think they are automatically on the same level as a pastry chef. It takes many years to learn to do what we do, and you *never* stop learning. There is so much more to running a bakery than just knowing how to decorate a cake! There is nothing more disrespectful than to hire someone to do a cake for you and then say you could have done a better job. All of my colleagues who I have told this story to all say that that is exactly what they will do on their last day on the job!

My wife, who was also cake decorator for a while says the same thing. She was a floral designer as well. You waste so much time with these indecisive customers who have no idea what they want, and you work so hard to go above and beyond their expectations only to have them turn up their noses or complain about something stupid like the color not matching the *exact* shade of the bridesmaid dress. People get a LIFE!

*Do not human beings have a hard service on earth, and are
not their days like the days of a laborer? Like a slave who longs
for the shadow, and like laborers who look for their wages, so
I am allotted months of emptiness, and nights of misery are
apportioned to me.*

*Job 7:1-3*

Most people don't realize how much time having your own business takes from you. I worked seven days a week, fourteen to eighteen hours a day. Working like that gets to you, but I really cared about my bakery and what I did.

The business was growing and we got paid very little. Yet the only way you can be successful is to work so hard. I don't think there is anything better in life than working for yourself and doing what you love, but there were days that I was very depressed.

I tried to tell my father that we should close at least on Mondays. He wouldn't hear anything about it. We were supposed to be partners, but in the end my dad always had the last word. He was the one who supposedly knew more than we did. Of course he was okay with *us* working seven days a week. He was hardly ever there!

When I was twenty, I began to get sick, really sick. I was losing weight like crazy, and I was losing my appetite. I was constantly in the bathroom because I always had to pee. In about two weeks I lost twenty pounds.

One evening I was making pies and it was one of those rare times my dad and I were in together. I guess he took a really good look at me.

"Something is really wrong with you", he said. "You've lost too much weight."

"I'm tired," I said.

"I'm taking you to the hospital right now."

Well, I didn't disagree. We went to the emergency department, and I ended up in the hospital for a week. The diagnosis was type I diabetes. It is very unusual to be diagnosed so late. Most people find out in their childhood, which is why it is sometimes called juvenile diabetes. The doctors wanted me to stay longer in the hospital, but I was determined to get out and back to work. I didn't want to leave my dad alone running the bakery.

No one else in my family has ever had type I diabetes. Part of me thinks that deep down I wanted to get sick just to get my dad to *see* me as a person and not just a work horse. Once I got Diabetes though, I was devastated. I remember confiding in my sister. How can I ever get married and have a family now? How can I put this burden on a woman and children? I felt like my life and dreams were done.

Now that I am married and have two beautiful children, I've had reason to reflect on the way things were. I think that back in my parents' time, people thought that life was always going to be hard and a struggle. I refuse to have that attitude. There is enough money out there for everyone to take a share. It isn't easy, and it requires work but it is possible to be successful. You have to teach your kids good values, and instill in them a positive attitude.

The things I want to instill in my children are these: You can do what you want in life. You can be rich if you want. Trust in yourself, trust in God. You can work for yourself and you can get married and be very happy if that is what you want! What was told to you as a child makes you the adult you are. The good news is that even if it was bad things you can change that!

If your parents put positive things into your life it is easier for you to live the life you want. Yet even if you had a hard life, a negative one with self-limiting beliefs and you've reached rock-bottom you can still succeed. You just need to believe in yourself. You need to work at it and you need to take action. Change the way that you think and erase those limiting beliefs. It is amazing how quick things can change when you are looking upwards. My life is great now and I never thought it would be! I had to surrender to my pain and let it go. I made a decision to live the life I wanted. You can too. Trust me, if I can do it, anyone can do it! My life was *hard*, but not today. Am I busy? Yes, but I am happy and my dreams are coming true. My home is paid and I have investments out there. Life is great! This is what I wanted and more.

Remember to never stop dreaming! You know the old saying the truth will sent you free. It is true, but be true to *yourself.* You deserve whatever you want and don't let anyone tell you differently.

My father does not have too much to say about me today, maybe because he is older, or maybe because he knew what he did wrong. Will he ever tell me? It is what it is, as long as I know what I want in my life, it won't matter.

One of my ideas for the bakery was to buy an assembly line to make the process of making buns faster. The dough goes through a hopper it cuts and rounds it into separate pieces and then the buns would then go through an overhead proofer and then dropped into a Kaiser machine where they were stamped. Then it only took one person to place them on a tray. My dad did not want to spend the money. It was too much, he said, when we had no guarantee the buns would sell. It took me a while to convince him, but I said we could write the cost of the machine off as a business expense and we would also be saving money on the labor. As well as that, we could guarantee sales by selling the Kaisers for ninety-nine cents a dozen. Which was ridiculously cheap even then. My line of thinking was that if people were coming in for the buns, they would end up buying deli as well. Also they would be able to see our cakes and pastries and remember us when they needed those things.

Eventually my dad had to give in over the logic of it. In the end he had to admit that it was well worth it. People would come all day and from all over town just to get the Kaiser sale. We had line ups out the door. We did a lot of other business just because of this special.

My dad never gave me credit for that idea though. To this day he still says it was his idea. I heard him talking to his friends and bragging about it.

Then we moved on to the pastries. We had a special for $9.99 a dozen. We would sell three thousand dollars' worth of pastries in a week. Today that would be around five thousand dollars. My dad wanted to have a special on the deli as well. So, deli, buns and pastries but never the cakes. We sold around two-hundred to three-hundred cakes a week. It varied from week to week. Everything worked hand in hand and the business was doing very well. At one point we were the largest independent business in Ontario. We won best bakery in the city three years in a row.

In 1988, we won an award for best European products and best customer services in all of Canada. The *Prime Minister* presented my dad with the award. When he accepted it, he never mentioned my brother or me. We have pictures from that day and Rocco and I aren't in any of them. That was my father, he wanted all the glory. It made me sick to my stomach. We were a family. I would never do that to my kids. I love them too much to set them aside like that. You should love your children and support them with their ideas and thoughts.

In the meantime, my father was getting worse and worse to work with. He was verbally abusive to me and my brother. It didn't matter how hard we were working, it was never enough. If anything we did was not perfect to his eye, it would be brought back and thrown in the garbage and whichever one of us was responsible would hear about it, in fact the whole store would hear about it! I must say that I didn't enjoy the way he talked to us, but he did make us understand that we had to have the best. When you are that young and still learning it hurts to be constantly insulted. A little encouragement would have helped out in between the abuse. When you constantly hear negativity over and over for fourteen years, it's hard to tune out. You start to think that maybe there *is* something wrong with you.

It wasn't just me, any of the decorators could get picked on. We used to do character cakes for kids' birthdays, up to thirty a week. I used to hate hearing him nitpick at everyone who had to do them.

I don't remember what year it was, but one year our accountant told us that we didn't make any money. Well, I could not believe that was true so I confronted my father. It didn't make any sense. Together we did some research and found out that the accountant was embezzling from us. He was immediately fired, but my dad would not let it go at that. He got back at that guy, and it wasn't by reporting him to the police! Many years later, he told us that he had him hurt, and bad. I don't know for sure whether or not this is true, but I think he was definitely capable of it.

In 1990, we were starting to see the money coming in and it was a nice change. We hired two new accountants. Hilary and Donald. They were very nice and they helped us a lot. My problem was that I was too involved with the business and I never had the time to help my dad with the paper work, so I never really realized just how well we were doing. Hilary and Donald organized the books and were showing all of us just how profitable La Roma was.

My dad went on a rampage with the money. He bought another house with land because he wanted to build his dream home. He went through cars like crazy; Audis, BMWs, Cadillacs, corvettes; whatever caught his fancy.

What bothered me was that he never had any intention of paying off the mortgage from the business. I always told him, let's pay the mortgage and then we can save some money to make investments out there in real-estate. My father already owned a six-plex and I was very proud of him that he had this property. I wanted to grow from that and buy another one. Each of us did buy a condominium. We put down ten-thousand dollars on each one. We rented them out with a one year leases.

All I ever wanted was a better life for my future and my future wife and kids. Is that so bad? I wanted to have enough investments out there, so that would take care of my future family *and* the business! What I wanted was to one day manage the business that I loved and keep it growing. As the years went by, I began to realize that my dad just wanted the business because he did not want to work. He had no problem enjoying the La Roma Bakery money. What upset me so much is that Rocco and I worked our asses off for our business because we *cared* about it. Dad only cared about the money.

My brother and I became very close to each other because of La Roma. We suffered together and we were happy together when things were going well. He is like me in that he wanted to be successful. It saddens me that we were not all on the same page because the bakery was doing very well and there was no excuse for *all of us* not be living a better life. We drew very little as a salary because we wanted the money to do more for the business. The friendship that we had, and still have, would help us both later in our lives.

Rocco and I would talk about what we thought was best for the business, but Dad would never listen. We worked so hard all the time, and watched him go on tropical vacations and buy cars with our money.

"It's obvious Dad is not sharing the profits of the Bakery with us," I said to him. "It's not right. We could do so much more with this place without him being so careless with all the money."

"If it wasn't for the old lady, all the money would be gone," Rocco said.

"What would you say about buying him out?" I asked.

"We can't do it ourselves."

"We can ask Mom to help us."

I approached my mother, and told her what our plans were. I told her what was happening and why we needed to get Dad out. At the time she agreed. She was not happy with how we were being treated either and she wanted us to be happy. At least that is what she said at the time.

We worked on presenting the case to our dad with the proposal to buy him out, but in the end my mother backed out. I was really angry at her, but I guess in the end she couldn't do it because it probably would have been the end of her marriage. Still, she wasn't losing anything by us working so hard. She had her husband at home and she was getting the high life Dad was providing with our share of the profits.

Rocco later confessed to me that he would steal from La Roma because he was angry that Dad helped us out so little while he enjoyed all the profits. I love my brother, but he *was* a little thief back then! With money, he is almost crazy, like he can't help himself.

I began to notice money missing from my wallet; just five dollars here, ten dollars there. Knowing my brother, I confronted him first, but Rocco can lie with a straight face and feel no remorse about it. I asked Nina, who was only sixteen at the time. She was upset that I even asked.

"Are you crazy? Go ask your brother!" she said. "You know it's him!"

So, in the backroom of the bakery I went to confront Rocco, who vehemently denied it over and over. His constant denials made me crazy.

"I know it was you!" I told him. "I don't care about the money! Just admit it!"

He just wouldn't budge! While our employees looked on, I grabbed him in a choke hold and squeezed tighter and tighter.

"I know you did it! Just admit it!" I shouted over and over again.

Rocco must have thought that one of our guys would step in and stop me, but I guess they must have been too much in shock! I watched Rocco's face turning red and then blue! *Finally,* Rocco garbled out something before he was about to pass out, and I let him go.

"Okay, I did it, I did it!" he was barely able to squeak out. He sat gasping on the floor for a few minutes.

"Sonofabitch! You almost fucking killed me!" he shouted.

"Never lie to me again!" I threatened him. "Or I *will* kill you!"

My poor staff! I must have scared them half to death. We laugh about this now, Rocco has changed a lot, but he's still cheap! If there is a penny on the ground, there is no way in hell Rocco is stepping over it.

Unfortunately, that incident was pretty much typical of my temper at the time. I don't think I was very emotionally stable back then. There was a time in the business that I just cracked. I went into a depression and did not understand what was happening. I just wanted to take a break.

I approached my dad. I told him that I wasn't well, I was sick and needed some time off. His response? He laughed in my face! Just laughed and walked away. He didn't take me seriously at all. If I had a chance to do it over again, I would have walked out right then and there. Why didn't I then? I don't know. I was too loyal to my family I guess. I wasn't just thinking about me, there was my brother and sister too. I can't help but wonder what life would have been like if I had gone out on my own. It would have been hard, very hard, but I could have done it. I ended up doing it anyway in the end.

My advice to any one stuck in a verbally abusive relationship, no matter if it is a parent or partner, GET OUT! You may think that it isn't hurting you but it is making your soul bleed, even if your body isn't.

What I was feeling during that time was misled, disillusioned and unable to trust. If my own father was such a liar how could I trust anyone else out there? I could not understand my father as a father; that he came first and we came second. He was never there for me, and didn't care about anything in my life that I wanted. He was a very negative man. There were times that I went crazy because of what he put into my head. I tried to confront him, but he just brushed me off because he knew that I loved him and would not let him down.

There were many nights that I went to bed feeling unappreciated. I would never treat any one like that. I always appreciated my staff and always thanked them for what they did for me. I always took care of them, paid them well and treated them well. They took care of me and the bakery and I am grateful for that. I always told my dad if you take care of your staff, they will take care of you. You need to make them part of the family. I was telling the wrong guy! Look how he treated his *actual* family!

*There is a vanity that takes place on earth, that there are righteous people who are treated according to the conduct of the wicked, and there are wicked people who are treated according to the conduct of the righteous. I said that this also is vanity. So I commend enjoyment, for there is nothing better for people under the sun than to eat, and drink, and enjoy themselves, for this will go with them in their toil through the days of life that God gives them under the sun.*

*Ecclesiastes 8: 14, 15*

The journey that I took at La Roma Bakery had its ups and downs. At the beginning we decided to focus on Italian goods and some Canadian goods. We did all kinds of Italian pastries. For example, tiramisu with Italian mascarpone, peach pastries, sospiri, cannoli's, hazelnut, bacio, and rum pastries. There was just so much that we did! Fruit tarts, eclairs and cream puffs in different formats. I also made an amazing cheesecake that had customers coming from all over. It was an easy recipe, but it was good. My brother-in-law would die for it! We also carried a variety of cakes: Italian rum, bacio cake, coffee cake, chocolate hazelnut and zabaglione cake, just to name a few. We also did all varieties of mousse cakes.

Our cookies were amazing. We made almond cookies, amaretto cookies, almond biscotti cookies, cut shortbread cookies and drop shortbread cookies and more.

I loved to be around that atmosphere because I enjoyed doing all kinds of everything. I also loved to create new items that were not on the market anywhere else. One of those things was an almond-apple puff pastry. Unfortunately, people from different bakeries would come to my store and try to copy the idea. That was fine with me, it just made me feel good that bakeries and supermarkets would use my ideas.

It was great that we were so busy, but sometimes I had to do cakes in the middle of the night because we were *that* busy and had no room. We did wedding cakes here and there, there was a big demand for it, but we just didn't have the space.

There was a decorator named Ingrid who wanted to come to work for us. She was good. She had won many awards for her work, but she wanted to learn more about the bakery business. We didn't need anyone at the time, but she was *very* persistent. She wouldn't give up. She was always coming in to look at our work and then to ask for a job. So I put her in once a week and eventually had her come in more often.

Ingrid worked on the truffles and the chocolate bark, and I taught her to do the pastries. We did a few wedding cakes together. It was nice working with her. You could tell that she had a passion for the work, and that she really wanted to be there. It is always good to be surrounded by people with that attitude. These are the kind of people that I like to hire.

As the bakery was growing, other people saw the success of La Roma Bakery and decided to open up a bakery close by. To be quite honest, our name was so strong that the competition didn't worry us too much. My father and I were talking to some sales people who told us that the bakery was going to open up across the street from us. We felt that this was a mistake on the part of the people opening it. It's one thing to open next to another small bakery but not next to one as big and successful as ours. Not only that, they had another location that was not doing well. I suppose they thought by moving next to us they would do well.

I felt bad for them but at the same time I felt disrespected too. These guys were coming in to try to take business from us after all. In Italy there are laws that prevent similar businesses from opening up next to each other in order to keep things fair. We approached them and told them politely that it was a mistake, but of course they didn't believe us. Some time went by and the same sales guys were telling us that the new guys were not doing so well.

Everything in life takes hard work. Nothing is easy. If it was, we all would be in business for ourselves and rich. There are leaders and there are followers, hard workers and not so hard workers. I feel bad that we shut down that bakery and there was a Bun World franchise not too far away that was there before we were that closed down too. I still feel bad about those stores, but what were we supposed to do? We were just protecting our store, and doing the best we could so customers chose us first.

We had been so careful picking out the location for our business. When we bought La Roma it was a *mess*, and it was really very hard work to build it up to what it was. It is kind of pathetic that some people think they can swoop in and just feed off your success. There's a misconception that just because you own your own business that you are rich. You certainly can be, but it doesn't happen overnight! Trying to poach someone else's hard work is not the way to go.

Some key things we did in our business was to hire specific people to fill specific rolls. We had a Polish pastry chef who made items that attracted a lot of eastern European people to the store. Also we had a Portuguese baker/pastry chef that was able to provide specific items for the Portuguese customers. We were not limiting ourselves only to Italian things. As we continued on we also starting to bring in more Canadian products. We were watching the community we were located in and trying to fill something for everyone.

I have to thank my dad for giving me the drive to be the best. People knew that when they came to our store they were getting good stuff, made with good quality. We did not cut corners just to go cheaper, like what seems to be happening more with bakeries opening up in places like Wal-Mart. I'm not putting down these places but at the end of the day, this is not high quality product. You get what you pay for.

In time we decided to open up a second bakery in a part of Mississauga that was being developed. We called it Maria's Bakery after my mom. It was a great location, right across the street from a brand new Portuguese church, and not too far from where we were living at that time.

We decided to partner with some family friends, Joao and Marisa. It worked out very well for everyone. We prepared most of the dough at La Roma and brought it to Maria's to be baked. Joao ran things at Maria's, making a salary plus half the profits from the bakery. It was making twelve thousand weekly, while La Roma was making twenty-three thousand. With both bakeries we had captured most of the business in that area. In the meantime at La Roma things were only getting busier. You would think we were running a manufacturing company with the amount we were selling, it was crazy.

Marisa was basically the manager of Maria's Bakery. She was a great manager and a great boss to the staff. It was impressive how organized she was. Also, she was such an honest person. We never had to worry about her stealing from us, or Joao either. They were such wonderful people. Joao came from a construction back ground, but he came a long way in the bakery business considering he knew nothing about it. We taught him everything, and he already understood all about working hard.

After three years my dad wanted to get out of Maria's. It wasn't bringing in the amount of money he wanted. Joao and Marisa did not want to run the bakery on their own, so the decision was made to shut it down. Joao went back into construction and he did alright so I am happy about that. Marisa decided to continue to work at La Roma Bakery. Since she did such a great job at Maria's Bakery, we decided to make her the manager. We had a manager previously but we found out she was stealing and had to fire her. We caught her stealing a block of mortadella. If you are going hungry, I have no problem feeding you or anyone. It is only the right thing to do. But I know this wasn't the case with this person. Marisa was *the best* manager and a great human being. Whatever she took, she paid for it. Even if we told her, she did not have to.

*A heart at peace gives life to the body, but envy rots the bones.*

*Proverbs 14:30*

My mother had a friend who was an employee of ours. She was a very beautiful woman and I think she had a thing for my dad. I am pretty sure she did! One day, one of our regular customers told me that she had seen my dad's Cadillac parked at the side of the store and this lady was in it with my father. Apparently, she was giving his balls a bit of a massage! My mother was furious, but my dad denies the incident.

"Don't be so suspicious," he said. "I was only giving her a ride to work. I can't help it that she made a pass at me. I told her to stop."

I didn't believe him but my mother did. Or at least she *wanted* to believe him and pretended she did. My father thought that because he had power and money he could do whatever he wanted.

I remember that we had a chartered accountant doing the year to date books and this woman was beautiful too. I don't know what happened, but he must have been flirting with her. One day she sent him a dozen roses out of the blue. My mother saw those roses and lost her mind.

"Where the hell did these come from?"

"Oh, the chartered accountant got them," Dad said.

"What for?" my mom fumed. "Are you doing *her* too?"

"You are so jealous!" my dad yelled back. "Just because a beautiful woman works for me doesn't mean I am fucking her! She's probably just saying thank-you for the business!"

"Well," says my mother, "If there is nothing is going on between you two, then you won't care if I say that I don't want her in this bakery anymore. Get rid of her."

So my dad had no choice but to get another accountant. But I have to say, if that had been my mother getting roses from a male accountant, my father would have killed him. My father did love my mother, but he also was very jealous.

One day in the bakery there were a few guys at the expresso bar and one of them was chatting up my mother. She didn't know that my father was in the office watching them on the cameras. After watching the banter back and forth he decided to come into the bakery and interrupt the conversation.

"Mary, come to the office I need to discuss something with you."

Once he got her into the office he ripped into her:

"What the fuck was that all about?"

My mom was shocked, "We were just talking out loud about our children and life," she said.

"Well I don't like it and you need to stop it," he said. "You don't need to talk to men like that. Just do your job."

So it was okay with him to flirt with the ladies, but my mother has an innocent conversation with another man and it is not allowed. It's not like my mother ever gave my dad reason to be suspicious, but he certainly gave her plenty of reason! Something is wrong with this picture!

I know what my mother saw in that customer. He was very charming, a great talker with a strong personality and he was also handsome. Mind you, my mother was very beautiful too, sweet and very old school when it came to attending my dad's needs. When my parents got married he was twenty-one and she was only eighteen. That is young, I was still learning the ups and downs of life at that age. I had a hard life and I'm thinking maybe because my parents' lives were hard they weren't going to make my life easy!

As time went by at La Roma Bakery, I can see that my father did not want us to have any of the money. I knew then my goal was to get out of the business, which saddened me because I loved working for myself and enjoyed doing what I was doing.

Interested business people had always approached us at La Roma Bakery asking if we would consider selling. We never even had to put it on the market. At end of it all we did sell and we were very pleased with what we received. We stayed there for month to train them and then we were gone. It really broke my heart to sell La Roma Bakery, but I had no choice. I had to get out of business with my dad because we are just too different from each other.

My advice to anyone, if you long for something, you should chase it. You may you even fail, but if that is want you want, try again! Set goals for your dreams and dates when you think you will be able to accomplish them. What you are doing is accomplishing your goals in stages. Once you are at that first stage then you focus on something else want in your life. You should never stop wanting to do better by yourself. It is just in you! If you are happy just doing a certain career, like being a nurse, there is nothing wrong with that, but if you have other things you want to do, do them!

*I hated all my toil in which I had toiled under the sun, seeing that I must leave it to those who come after me—and who knows whether they will be wise or foolish?*

*Ecclesiastes 2: 18, 19*

We talked to our real estate agent to look for a property with a bakery and he found us a power of sale. It was a six thousand square feet bakery. It was a big! It used to be a business that did mainly wholesale. The bakery was very run down, but because it was a power of sale, the price was right and we had the money to fix it. It was sure was a good deal! There was also a house on the property. One thing about my father and me, we weren't afraid of taking chances. It was almost was like it drove us. That is one way that we are alike.

The new bakery did fine right from the get go because of our reputation at La Roma Bakery. A lot people from that neighborhood came to our bakery. I'm not trying to be conceited, but we were very well liked in the bakery world. We did all the renovations and the bakery looked beautiful and we called it La Prima Bakery. We were covering our expenses and making some money. Which was better than we did at La Roma Bakery in the beginning.

At La Prima Bakery we had a little of a different approach. The area was a good location because most people living there were debt free. They had more money to spend. That is good for the bakery business because then it was fair price with good margins.

Our oven was a thirty shell oven. It was big! I never worked with such a big oven before, it was quite an experience. You had to time everything perfect for the breads and buns, or you would burn them.

That would go the same with any of the puff pastry goods, cakes, breakfast items and cookies.

One day I was working with my pastry chefs, Sal and Nick. We were doing cakes and desserts. All of a sudden I felt unwell. I knew something was wrong but it was too late for me to call out or do anything about it. I passed out on the floor. It seemed like from a distance I could still hear people talking. I think the guys were worried.

"Just work around him, he's dead. Or sleeping." I heard my brother say.

In the meantime I was in a hypoglycemic coma! I would've died if I had been left too long! My dad came down the stairs, shook me and asked me what he should do. I managed to tell him to get me some juice. Thank God for my dad that day, or maybe I would be dead!

The first thing I did when I came around was chase my brother to give him a good pounding!

"You fucker!" I said, "Like I'm going to take a nap on the floor!"

The guys, who I guess were used to my outbursts by now, just carried on as usual!

The bakery was doing very well and the money was there. Did I see any of it? The answer would be no! My father had not changed, the same old guy being very generous with our money for his needs and whomever else he felt should enjoy it. It came to a point where I had enough.

"I'm sick of this shit. It's killing me," I said. "Either you buy me out or sell the bakery."

"The bakery is still too new to sell," he protested. I knew he was going to say that.

"Then you got no choice but to shut it down. Because I am *done*."

"I won't! I'll buy you out."

I knew in my heart that he was lying. He would never put money in my hands because he would lose the power to control me. In the end he decided that we would close the bakery. I didn't want to close it, but it had to be done so Rocco and I could get free. I think we could have sold it and then we would have had something to show for it. In 1999 we closed up shop and divided the land in three lots to sell. When all was said in done, I got out of the business with twenty dollars in my pocket and a big fat zero in my bank account. I couldn't understand it.

When I confronted my dad and asked where Rocco and my share was, he said that we didn't make any money on the sale.

"The money we made on the sale went to pay off the mortgage," he said.

"Whose mortgage? The bakery's or yours? Or is it in your bank account?"

"It had to go to the debt," was all that he would say.

My heart was broken. My portfolio of cakes I threw in the garbage and I said I would never be a pastry chef ever again.

*How long, O Lord? Will you forget me forever? How long will you hide your face from me? How long must I bear pain in my soul, and have sorrow in my heart all day long?*

*Psalm 13:1*

Since the day that I was out of the business, my feeling towards my dad was pure hate. It was not good for me, but I could not help feeling that way. I took a month off just to rest. Afterwards sent off my resume to three supermarkets. I wanted to work for the big chain supermarkets because they had benefits which I needed badly.

My brother and I were approached by the owner of the Bun World franchises. He wanted to hire us both to grow his business because he losing so many stores. He wanted my brother to manage the bread and buns and me to work the cakes and kinds of other desserts. We agreed to do it, but we wanted a contract done up. He said he wanted to see how went at the beginning and if it went well and then he would offer us a contract. There was no way we were going to put the work in to fix up somebody else's business just have them tell us to take a hike after! We said sorry, no contract, no deal.

In the meantime all three supermarkets had called me. One of the bakery managers, Luke had recognized my name. He had supplied us with sponge cake at La Roma when we were too busy to make our own. He put in a good word for me to the bakery merchandiser and the store manager. With him acting as a reference for me I got top pay. A week later the Bun World guy calls me saying he was willing to offer us a contract. Rocco and I both had secured good jobs by then so he was out of luck.

I needed to work because I had nothing to my name. It was very hard for me to work for someone else. I was very depressed and angry at the same time. Most of the time I just put an act on for my staff and the people I worked around. I *was* happy because of the pay and at least I was the boss of my own department. It was not easy though, when you have be working for yourself for so long, you can understand. My manager supported all my decisions. She had faith in me on how to run a department because of my background.

It's funny because in business and now being a department head you always have one guy that thinks he can do a better job. The thing is when you work for a supermarket it is different. I find people just treat it like a job, but they do not care as much because it is not theirs. Either that or they take it way too serious like the company can't run without them.

This one particular person thought he could run the department. So I challenged him. It's yours for a week. He backed off. Every person thinks the grass is better on that side. They don't know all the responsibility you have and to make sure things run as smooth as possible. When it's their own ass on the line, the tune usually changes.

We had a lot of ladies working in that store. I sure loved the ladies. But I told everyone that I do not mix business with pleasure. I sure wanted to sometimes, but I didn't. I knew my decorator Kerrie had the hots for me. She was already taken, but I think she would not have minded doing the tango. If you know what I mean! I would never have an affair with any woman that was married or had a boyfriend. Mind you, she was hot!

It is funny how your staff challenges you. Kerrie was very feisty. She was always testing the waters with me and apparently one day I had enough and I called her a bitch. For the life of me I *do not* remember saying that! In my defense, she must have really been breaking my balls for me to do it. *Five* years later when she decided to move to another store, she approached me and confronted me about that day. I asked her why she didn't say something the day that it happened. I would have apologized then! She was a great decorator and still a friend today. Though I have not seen her for a while, just because I am so busy with work and family.

I was doing well in my department, increasing sales which is what the big wigs wanted from me. I did four thousand dollars a week. My department was one of the top stores for sales increases. Not bad for a store that did not have much overall sales.

How did I do it? The secret is customer service. The customer is like gold! In retail business, if you take care of the customer, people will talk about it and bring friends with them too. That's it! Yes, you should do good products and it should presentable, but the key is to take care of the customer. I won best customer service at my store. That says a lot!

There were good days and bad days. My first issue as a department head was with the produce manager, Rich. Usually he was a real nice guy. He wanted to use one of my girls, Joanne, in his department and I told him he could not use her that day because I needed her. He started to argue with me. I told him to get out of my department and he did not take it very well. I told him that if he had an issue we can take this outside and I would put him thirty feet under. Joanne was in the bakery with me at the time and she was in the middle of the fight. She ran out of the department because she was afraid! Rich finally walked away and the next day there was a bowl of fruit in my department and he apologized. I said no problem, and things went back to normal. I got a reputation that no one should try to fuck with me.

I was in the right, but I did not handle it well. So why did I react like a mad man? That is easy to answer, it's because I was not happy with my life situation. I feel badly about what I did because that is not in my heart. I would like to say I'm sorry to Rich and Joanne. I was very angry and I would overreact on anyone. Can you believe that Joanne would marry me seven years later? I'm so sorry Babe! Sometimes I think I am so lucky to have her because most women would not be able to handle a guy like me at that time.

When Joanne started to work for me, she had transferred in from another store that was closing, and she worked quite some time in the department before I ever met her in person. We talked on the phone now and then but that was it. I was expecting a bit of a bitch, because I had some bad experiences with people from her old store, but she was nice enough. I remember her saying she was pleasantly surprised by me, because she had some pretty nasty bosses. Some guys who worked in the store were always asking me who the hot new girl was. I was dying to see her, one day!

It was around this time that I started dating Alisha. We had been chatting online for a few months before we met in person. She was a little reluctant to get out in the dating scene again as she was recently divorced and didn't want to end up with another jerk. Her husband really didn't appreciate her as a woman. She was more of a chattel to him. She was looking for romance, and I certainly appreciate romance! Even my most short term relationships were treated to my romantic side. So I suppose we connected on that level.

Alisha and I got along really well. I was able to open up to her and tell her a lot of the problems I had with my father.

"This is such a sad thing," she said, "I see this so often. So many people have a poor relationship with their father. I see it with my sons too. I don't think they will ever be close to their dad."

"If I ever have kids," I said, "I would never, *ever* treat them that way."

"You would be a great father," she said. "Look how much my boys love you."

"Look how much they love *you*," I answered. "You did a very good job raising them. They are so polite and respectful. That's a credit to you."

Not to take anything away from all the great dads out there, but the world sure would be a better place if fathers nurtured their sons better. I figure that a child's (boy or girl) model for manhood is their father. If you have a father that treats his wife and kids poorly, there you have kids that think that is "normal" male behavior. It isn't! A *real* man takes care of his family first and would do anything for them. A man who shows his son that he loves his mother, and loves him too, creates a loving man who has respect for women and others when he grows up.

I guess all this talk about parenthood had Alisha thinking about a real future with me, and possibly making *me* a father for the first time. I sure would have loved to have kids. At that time in my life I was really hoping that someday that would happen.

We had a relationship that lasted about two years. To have spent that time with her was an honor. I can't remember any of that time being bad. I used to think that this was too good to be true. She was just happy to be happy. She enjoyed my company and didn't expect a ton in return. My model of marriage was not a good one. All my parents did was fight. Even most of my past relationships involved a lot of arguing, but Alisha and I never argued.

I could see in Alisha's eyes that she was making plans for a life with me. She wanted to travel all over the world; Australia, Switzerland and Italy. We talked about it a lot. I really would have liked to have taken those trips with her, but I couldn't lead her on anymore. She was looking for a man to spend the rest of her life with, and as much as I cared for her, I did not love her. God, I *wish* I did! Very rarely do you meet a person like Alisha. She was beautiful, thoughtful and intelligent. She had such a sparkle in her eye. When I think of a class act, I think of Alisha.

We were lying together in bed one night when she told me how she felt.

"I'm falling in love with you, Bruno."

"I love you too." I said. I can honestly say that I meant it, but it wasn't in the way that she really would have wanted. The time had come for me to come clean. Afterwards I had to tell her the truth.

"Alisha, you know, I do love you, but not in the way you deserve," I said.

It broke my heart to tell her that! I hated causing her that much pain. But it would have been more unfair to carry on that way knowing how she felt. Some guys just stay with a woman they don't love and suddenly dump her when they find someone else. I think that's despicable. That's just using someone at the expense of their feelings.

What more can I say? She was graceful to the very end, she could have screamed and called me every name in the book, she could have told me to get the fuck out of her house. But like I said, she was class. It might have been easier for me if she had have done all those things. It killed me to see her cry, knowing it was my fault.

"I hope you find the woman you are looking for," she told me.

"Listen Alisha," I said. "I know someday you will make a man very happy. One day you will meet a guy who loves you and appreciates you. There are good guys out there."

What the hell was wrong with me? I don't know! She was too good for me. I don't mean that in a bad way. I just think we didn't connect on a passionate level. I can't help but think on that Eagles song *One of These Nights*:

*"I've been searching for the daughter of the devil himself. I've been searching for an angel in white. I've been waiting for a woman who's a little of both and I can feel her but she's nowhere in sight."*

Did such woman actually exist? I would eventually find out!

The time came where Joanne was finally able to work days and I needed a clerk to work alongside me in the day time. When she walked through those bakery doors, I thought, "Ouch! It's going to hurt me working with this one!" What a cutie with long auburn hair and big blue eyes. She was *very* attractive and she was also very sweet and easy to work with.

She was a good worker too. When I told her what she needed to do she said:

"That's it? I can get that done in less than four hours."

"Yeah, okay," I laughed.

"No really," she said, "If I can get this done in less than four hours can I sit the rest of the shift and read my book?"

"If you can do that, you are more than welcome to sit and read your book!"

Well, she was as good as her word! But after a while she started feeling guilty about sitting around and doing nothing. She wanted to learn what she could. I trained her to do the mix and buns, and Kerrie and I started to show her how to do the cakes. I think Kerrie was jealous of her, but they got along well. Joanne was like that, always nice to people until they gave her reason not to be.

I used to flirt with her all the time, but we had some really good conversations too. She understood my negativity towards my father because she had a rough go with her father too.

"My dad was verbally abusive too," she told me. "He said a lot of hurtful things to my mother when he was angry. When I was a teenager he practically ignored me. When he was mad he would call me a stupid bitch or tell me to fuck off. It was hard to take. I thought he hated me for a long time."

She was able to forgive him though, because she understood better the upbringing that he had and the stress he was under at the time. At least she knew *why*. I just didn't know *why* with my dad! He never talked about his childhood, he never wanted to. I wondered if I would be able to forgive him if he would.

One day, there was a huge snow storm and it was like a ghost town in the supermarket. Joanne and I were sitting in the back room just chatting it up because there was nothing else to do. I told her about a time I got stuck in a big snow storm on the way to a concert in Buffalo.

"Buffalo! Good god," she said. "Was it worth it?"

"Oh yeah, it was amazing!"

"Who did you see?"

"Well, you probably never heard of them," I said, "A rock band called Triumph."

"Oh my god! I *love* them!" she cried. From then on, she would bring her little tape recorder to work and we would listen to Triumph and all sorts of rock bands at work.

I just *knew* that she was the one. There was a big problem, though. She was *married*! What should I do? I asked God. If she really is the one, I will leave it in Your hands. In the meantime I had a new girlfriend, but I wanted Joanne more.

After a while it got easier for me because Joanne decided to go back to school. She always wanted to be in health care, and she had enough of her husband bitching at her to make more money. So she was only working the odd evenings and weekends and I hardly ever saw her anymore.

I also enjoyed managing the store on Sundays. It brought back memories with my business, making sure everything was running smoothly.

With Joanne gone, I needed a new decorator and also new part-time clerk. So this twenty-one year old beautiful blondie with green eyes applies for the job. So I hired her! Nobody in the department liked Brook because they thought I hired her just because of the way she looked. I won't lie, it didn't hurt! We did have a lot in common too. She liked rock music, she wanted to study to be a director and I was ready with a script that I called "Eyes Watching".

One day she asked me if I would go out with her. I told her that if we did she would have to keep it a secret from everyone. God bless her, she did too! She never even told my wife. If she wanted to be a bitch she could have. But she and Joanne always got along well. Joanne even made sure Brook was invited to our wedding.

Brook and I had the one date only. I *swear* I was a gentleman! She was just too young for me, it didn't feel right. I wouldn't have married her anyway because I didn't feel that way about her. But she was very attractive! We were good friends and she was very nice. I also liked her because she was part Irish and Italian. What a mix! It seemed I had a problem in that store because so many ladies there were interested in me. What to do? I had my fun, but I kept my distance.

*No discipline seems pleasant at the time, but painful. Later on, however, it produces a harvest of righteousness and peace for those who have been trained by it.*

*Hebrews 12:11*

The pain in my heart that I had with my dad was just getting bigger. I talked to Joanne a lot about him and to my brother every day. If you remember earlier I mentioned that we would be closer as brothers but also as business partners. We decided to buy our first home together, right across from a College. We rented it out to two professors for five years. They were great, never missed the rent and were very good tenants.

My father was so against us buying the house and renting it out. He said we would have nothing but headaches. He owned the six-plex for twenty-two years and he had problems all the time. I look at it like this, it is how you decide to handle the situation you are in. I used to pray to God to help me. I never had any problems with any of the investments I had. Thank you God!

My father was so negative, or he did not want us to be successful. I just do not understand why! It sometimes drives me crazy! I love my dad, even though he hurt me real bad. I wouldn't want anyone to experience what I have experienced.

Thanks to my wife, I am much better now. She helped me to understand that I cannot change my father, but only accept him for who he is. I just want to say *I love you* and I don't understand what happened in your past to make you the way you are.

A year and a half later my brother and I bought another house. I was determined to be successful. Even though I had already had a successful business and I came out of there with nothing. Of course, it bothered my dad. Why, I cannot answer that, but my life was getting back on track. Life was finally getting good again, and didn't seem so hard all the time. My heart was still in a lot of pain though and I still hated my father. I prayed to God to help me with the pain in my heart. I didn't want to feel like that any longer, but it was there.

I was eating dinner with my family and we were all talking about different bakeries and the owners and who was doing well or not. We came around to La Roma Bakery and how well the store was doing.

"If you had listened to me," my dad said, "You would have been millionaires by now."

"Are you kidding me?" I yelled. "You spent all the money and you stole from me and Rocco! We aren't millionaires *because* we listened to you and trusted you!"

"If that's how you feel then maybe I should just take you out of my will!"

"Keep your damn money, I don't need it. If you're done with me, I'm done with you. You are nothing but a liar, you always came first and everything you do is just to show off to strangers! You don't care what *your own family* thinks about you!"

My brother told me that my dad actually did go to his lawyer and had me taken out of his will.

"Well that says a lot about how he really feels about me." I said.

My brother never talked back to my father. But I just couldn't take all the bullshit anymore. I mean, how *dared* he claim that he wanted to see us rich when he had been stealing from us all that time? I didn't care if I never spoke to him again. I was so angry.

We did not see each other for a while and one day my sister approached me and asked if I would come back and make the family whole again. I told her I didn't know if we could ever be a real family, but I would come back and try to be civil. I never did get an apology, but apparently I am back in the will again, according to Rocco. Whatever, I have to accept that my father will never admit that he had done anything wrong to us.

Getting back to my job it was going well, but it was different from any other jobs I had. I never worked a union job before. They are there to protect our wages and our jobs, and I appreciate that, but sometimes that means people think that they can fuck the dog all day.

I have seen people come and go. I guess they have their place there. I had a great staff that took care of each other and I thought that was great. I would do anything for them and protect them. I always seemed to have problems with the people outside of my department though. I was willing to work with them, but some of them thought their shit didn't stink. I think a great leader is one whose staff loves them, but also respects them.

There was a situation with the new meat manager. Joanne would bring the racks of raw buns and pastries to the meat fridge for storage and the baker would take them out the next morning. We had always done this, the old manager even made space for us just to put our racks. So Ed storms in and starts giving Joanne shit for doing something that was always okay for her to do before. First of all it was not in anyone's way and there was plenty of room for them to move around and get the meats. He tells her to bring the racks back to the bakery department.

"But Bruns, where the hell am I supposed to put them?" she said.

"What is the problem here?" I confronted him. "We always put it there with the old manager."

"I'm the manager now, this is my department and my cold room," he said.

"So where do you want me put them, up my ass?" I yelled at him. He was still giving me a hard time, so I told him I am leaving it here and if you have a problem let's take it out back. He backed down and the racks stayed.

After that day he never spoke to me again. I feel that most department heads had a chip on their shoulder. It is just a job they are doing. Great you have that title, but you're not god. I got along with anyone that respected me. Respect was a big thing in our family. If you dis-respect, then there will be problems. If you're wrong, it will not go well. If I am wrong, then I will say I am wrong.

My staff loved me because I took care of them when there was trouble with our department heads. I was not there to be a hero, I was there to do a job. I find a lot people in the work force are on power trips. If people put down other people it is because of their own insecurity. People should be good to each other.

How would you feel if people are talking trash about you? Some say it does not bother them, but you know it is not true. I am the kind of person that I am nice to everyone because they are human just as I am. But I do have a temper when people do not want to work together, as you can see.

*Set me as a seal upon your heart, as a seal upon your arm; for love is strong as death, jealousy is cruel as the grave. Its flashes are flashes of fire, a most vehement flame. Many waters cannot quench love, neither can floods drown it. If a man offered for love all the wealth of his house, it would be utterly scorned.*

*Song of Solomon 8: 6-7*

I remember Joanne telling me about her husband who was not treating her very well. Whenever he was done with his latest fling, he wanted to work it out with her. I tried to be positive with her, trying to help her make it work. She had tried so many times and he seemed to think it was her who had to do all the changing. He wanted to go to a counselor, but Joanne was already done. He was very upset, but he just wanted her as a safety net.

I guess one day she had enough of sitting home alone. That Friday at work I was sitting doing the inventory while she was decorating cakes. She turns to me and says:

"So what are you doing tomorrow night?"

"Why? You want to go out with me?" I joked.

"Don't joke, I'm serious!" she said and turned back to her work.

I was in shock! I was happy, but I was supposed to go out with my girlfriend that Saturday night. But I *really* liked Joanne and I wanted to go out with her. I came up with some excuse and cancelled my date. I felt horrible about what I did to my girlfriend, but I couldn't let this opportunity pass me by.

We went out to a club in Toronto and we had *a lot* of fun. I just felt comfortable with her. She was shy with me but she was also wild. I don't know if that makes any sense, but that's what it was like. We had a lot in common, but we are also opposites in a lot of ways too. Which is good because it makes our relationship interesting.

Staying focused at work was really hard after that. Every minute we had we were fooling around. One day I was sitting back for a break as she was pulling racks from the oven.

"Come here, Babe" I said, pointing to my lap.

"Bruns, we're supposed to be *working*," she said.

"Ah come on," I pleaded, and pleaded ...

"No."

"Really? I waited five years for you and now you won't even sit on my lap? If you don't come here I'll come and get you!" I threatened.

Joanne went white. She knew I was serious! But I really wouldn't have done anything if she didn't want it.

"Oh, *alright*," she laughed. "But not here. We need a better spot."

It wasn't all fun and games though. Her ex made it very hard for her to leave. It was weird, first he wanted her out and then he was mad at her for leaving. He was always calling and threatening her and calling her horrible names. Joanne was afraid of him for a very long time. When she finally broke down and called the cops he backed off, but he still made it hard for her in court. We would be married for two years and have a child before it was finally all finished. What a waste of time.

In the meantime, we had so much fun together. We went all over, Niagara Falls, Toronto Islands; wherever we wanted. We talked for hours about everything. When we weren't together we were yapping on the phone. Even when we were just sitting watching TV together it was nice. I would stay with her for days and she would stay with me a few nights too.

"You may as well just move in," she laughed one day, and eventually that is just what happened.

My family wasn't crazy about her at first. I guess because she was divorced, they thought that she would eventually leave me. Or maybe it was because it had been a *long* time that I brought a woman home to meet them, and I was spending all my time with her and not with them. It annoyed me because I thought they would be happy for me.

After about a year I guess they were accepting her more, because they invited us both to come to Italy with them that summer. Joanne was thrilled because she had always wanted to go to Italy.

While we were in Italy, my dad approached Joanne and asked her;
"Do you really love my son?"

"Well yes, John, of course I do," she replied.

"Then please take care of him," my dad said. "He doesn't eat well or take care of himself like he should."

"I'll do my best, but you know how stubborn he is."

I don't know what he was trying to do, if he was genuinely concerned for my health, or just trying to make himself look like a loving father to Joanne. If he cared so much about my health, why didn't he treat me better when I got sick in the first place?

But getting back to Joanne, I used to write so many love letters to her and woo her, when I asked her to marry me she had no choice but to say yes. I will never forget when I proposed to her, I bought her twelve dozen roses and had a little note with each dozen of roses. I also had a calendar made for her with photos of us together and the last photo was me on my knee with the ring in my hands. She didn't give me a chance to propose, she just said yes. That was the happiest day of my life.

I don't suppose my family thought it would last so long. They were always talking about money and situations where women take all the money during a divorce. That definitely wasn't Jojo! She was just trying to get away from her ex! Joanne finally put that nonsense to rest one day.

"Bruno's money is Bruno's money!" she said. "What he has saved up till now has nothing to do with me. If he wants me to sign a prenuptial, I'll sign a prenuptial!"

I never made her sign anything, I know she would have if I asked. It was not in her nature to try and cheat anybody.

When I met Joanne, my life changed for the better. She was trying so hard to help me deal with my pain. She saw the anger that I had against my father. She understood what I had gone through. She knew how much I loved my bakery, but there was no going back.

My dad was happy that I was finally getting married. He wanted more grandchildren, especially a Deluca boy to carry on the family name. He was very friendly to Joanne, maybe a little too friendly!

It didn't matter what the conversation was, my dad always managed to steer it towards sex. Maybe he got a kick out of making her blush, or maybe I was too happy and he was trying to mess things up for me.

We were enjoying a weekend at my parents' trailer when my dad dropped this bomb on her.

"Who do you think would last longer in bed, me or Bruno?" he asked her.

"What do you mean?" Joanne blurted out, almost choking on her drink.

"I bet he doesn't go very long," he said.

Flabbergasted, Jojo looked helplessly at me. I just rolled my eyes and shook my head. I didn't know what to say either.

"Well?" my dad pushed.

"I think I'm not very comfortable talking about this with my future father-in-law," she said.

"Come on, who do you think lasts longer?"

"Well, John, you are twenty years older than him!"

"That's got nothing to do with it! Just answer the question!"

I wasn't going to let Jojo go through this any longer.

"Maybe we should ask Mom what she thinks," I said.

My mother who had been buzzing around the table serving lunch just grunted and rolled her eyes. Thankfully that put an end to that awkward conversation.

"What the hell was that all about?" Joanne asked me after. "I mean *come on!*"

"That's just him trying to compete with me and be better than me," I said. "Nothing is sacred, not even my own bed."

"Did he *really* think I was going to say he would be better?" she laughed. "The guy is like sixty-five!"

"Who knows how that guy thinks? I never understood him."

*For the love of money is the root of all evils; it is through this craving that some have wandered away from the faith and pierced their hearts with many pangs.*

*1 Timothy 6: 10*

My dad and I do have a lot of things in common. We both have the drive to succeed. We are both stubborn and we both like to be in charge. The difference between us is that my dad doesn't know what to do with his success to hang on to it. He spends so much money, almost just for the sake of spending it!

I remember my mom said we would get some money but I never saw anything come my way. My dad told my brother that he would give us fifty-thousand dollars each. Still waiting! Once he said he would give each of us three-thousand a month. Where is that? Still hasn't happened! I thank God that I had a roof over my head and food on the table when I was younger. I had nothing to complain about until we became business partners and he lied to me.

My father always wanted to look like a big shot. I asked my uncle if he had always been like this. He said no, he was a real good guy. When I heard that tears came running down my face. My heart was broken because I can see him actually being a great guy to be around. When his mother was alive she used to tell him that money was not everything, but I guess he didn't pay attention to that advice.

My father always wants to project this image to other people. I don't understand why he cares what other people think. Isn't the opinion of your family has about you more important? He was a good human being at one time.

My father looks at other people's lives and wants what they have, but I always say they have what they got by hard work and understanding on how to make money. Life is not just about money. It says in the bible that money is the root of all evil! That is only if that is all you think about and if you have money you should use it to help others. If you help others you are helping yourself too! What do I mean? Again there is an old saying what goes around, comes around.

One day my bakery merchandiser approached me and said that I would have to leave the store because someone with more seniority was bumping in. So, off I go again, but I was looking forward to it. I was hoping the change would be a good one. I ended up with a nice big department. The staff was happy to have me. Apparently the last manager was not a very good one. She had told everyone that I wouldn't be able to handle the department.

"Oh please," I said. "I ran my own business for years. You think *one* department in going to bother me?"

I wanted to know how they had been doing things. I listened to them, and they listened to me when I wanted things changed. I rearranged the shifts, changing two part time shifts into one eight hour shift. We ended up making more cakes that way. I also I trained any of the clerks who were willing to learn to do cakes, so that we would never be short of a decorator in case of emergency.

My reputation had preceded me though. My old produce manager nemesis Rich, had been working there before me, and I guess had warned everyone about me! Maybe that explains why everyone was so darn nice at first!

As time went by my staff was feeling comfortable with me. But Roxanne, the head decorator was not easy to work with. She had her opinions, but at the end of the day I did what I thought was best. I used say this in my business and I said it there. Let's all just get along and have some fun. I understand that it could not like that every day because we all have bad days, but at end of it all we need to be civil.

One day Roxanne was not happy with her part time help and she was stressed out, so I offered to help her to do the cakes. She explodes and says to me that if we traded spots, that she could do a better job.

"Oh please Honey, I can do your job and mine and with my eyes closed. Pick a week," I said. "And I'll let you try." Most people react like that because of problems that they are having in their own life.

She backed down, embarrassed and never said a word again. In order to be a good leader, if your staff challenges you on anything, you have to call them on it. So they know who is boss. After that we were good friends.

Everyone in my department came to my wedding. All the staff knew Joanne, they would talk to her on the phone when she called and they would say we are watching him for you!

Unfortunately, there is always one trouble maker in every department. Amanda was a part timer. She was always stirring things up and trying to turn people against each other. The world is full of so many people who get their kicks by causing shit. Amanda didn't like taking orders very well, but when you have a job, you do things the way the boss wants them done. That's what you're getting paid for. Sometimes when there is a union, people think that means they can do whatever they want and not get fired. It's not always easy to get it done, but it can be done. I got sick of her big mouth and let her have it. As I was turning my back, she shot me the finger, but I saw her do it.

"All right honey, if that's the way you want to play."

I had her written up, and eventually she was fired.

She was going back and forth with the union to get her job back. Nobody wanted her back because she thought she could do what she wanted. She met the wrong guy when she came across me. I'm not trying to sound tough, but it drives me crazy when people think they can do whatever they want and get away with it because the union is going to defend them. She was a wild one, now put in her place.

At the end of it all they took her back and sent her to another store if she wanted it. I heard through the grape vine, she is well behaved. That's the way she should have been from the start.

At this time my brother and I decided to buy a house together to live in. It was a new townhome and we were so happy because we were doing very well in our lives. I was thirty-seven. Four years earlier I had only the twenty dollar bill in my pocket. Now we had three homes and money invested in the stock market. So you can imagine, fourteen years in business what could have accomplished if we had been allowed. I always hear it is too hard to be rich. Why? If that is what you want in your life, you can have it.

I remember Rocco and me in that townhome. That house was spotless. Not a speck of dirt. If I was having my dinner in the kitchen and I dropped some crumbs on the floor, he would pick it up. He would drive me crazy because he would get mad if any crumbs fell on the floor.

Jojo and I were watching a movie one evening and he was picking up the pieces of popcorn around us.

"How can anyone relax with this guy buzzing around?" she said. "Let's watch movies at my house from now on!"

In the morning when she was trying to get ready for work, she couldn't find her make-up case.

"I swear I left it on the bathroom counter!"

We finally found it put away under the sink. OCD Rocco had struck again.

"Tell your girlfriend not be such a slob," he retorted when I asked him why he touched her make-up case in the first place.

"She was only staying one night! You want to give her own closet?"

That was the last night she stayed over. She told me I cannot handle your brother. He is a neat freak! I told her he got that from my mother. When she came to my mother's house, she saw the similarities.

Jojo was drinking a take-out coffee in the living room and *three* times my mother came around to throw the cup away. Finally she lost her patience.

"I'm not finished that! I'll throw it away when I'm *done!*"

My parents' place is spotless too, it's like a damn museum. It's funny because whenever my kids are there, my mother is all over them because their toys are everywhere. I had to tell her they are just kids! Please Mom let them play in peace!

My brother is now living with my parents again, and even he says she is crazy with all the crumb picking and complaining.

"Bruno, she drives me nuts!" he said. "She never leaves me alone."

"Well, why do you think she's like that?" I asked. "It's obvious that she's not happy."

"What has she got to be pissed off about? She has everything!" Rocco said. He thought about it a little more and then he added, "You know, Dad told me that she had been depressed. That once she had an episode that lasted about two years. I still don't get it."

"What's not to get?" I said. "Look who she's married to! She wasn't like that when we were kids. All the shit he put her through. It was her that got hurt, not him! Have you ever really listened to how he talks to her?"

"I never thought about it that way," he said. "I guess that's why she takes it out on everything around her, but that doesn't help anything. Dad bugs me too but I don't let it bother me."

"She's not at peace, Rocco," I said. "Try to remember that when she's acting crazy."

How many times I went crazy in my life, not understanding the pain in my heart. I was so angry, and I took it out on other people. I mean, I was nuts! I could be a real bastard. I didn't really want to be that way though. I asked God to get me through it. My father was so cold towards me and my brother. I did not get it. I get it now. It was about how he looked towards the public. I don't care how I look towards the public. You be good to your fellow human beings just for the sake of being good, not for looking good.

In my opinion, as a parent you should be listening to your child. Hear what they are saying. Help them with their dreams, even if it does not make sense to you. It is about their happiness. Don't be like my father that was trying to control me instead of having a relationship with me.

I was at Niagara Falls with my wife and I saw a father with his son. He must have been around ten years old. His father was hugging him and asking him if he was having fun. I should have minded my own business, but I could not help but see the love that he was giving his son. The boy responded, "Dad I love you and I am having so much fun."

They were hugging each other and smiling. At that moment tears came to my eyes. I thought, *there* is a father that loves his son! Seeing his needs and serving him. My heart dropped to the floor. I did not want my wife see how I was reacting because we were on vacation and she was happy. It was a beautiful moment seeing this love between a father and a son. That is how it should be, so when they become adults they are a well-developed human being.

There is an old saying in the Bible, do unto to others, as you would want done to you. Can you imagine if each of us would be a little more compassionate towards each other, the kind of world it would be. All I have to say about that is one word, LOVE. I am not perfect, but I try each day to be a good human being and help anyone that needs help at that moment. In this world too many people are jealous and they just think about themselves.

*Your wife will be like a fruitful vine within your house; your children will be like olive shoots around your table.*

*Psalm 128: 3*

Joanne and I had been together for four years, including the two years we had been dating. There was still no sign of a little one coming and we were starting to accept the fact that maybe it wasn't in the cards for us. Jojo had always thought that she couldn't have children. She had been with her ex for seven years and nothing had happened.

We agreed that if we couldn't do it naturally then we wouldn't do it at all. So when Joanne said she would like to go to a fertility clinic I was a bit annoyed.

"I'm not looking for anything artificial," she said. "I just want to see if anything is wrong. Then I can at least have some peace of mind and stop getting depressed every thirty days!"

Little did I know that would include testing for me too! Awkward! But I really wanted kids and I loved my wife so I went through the brief romance with the little jar. I was nervous too. As a man, you don't want to think that maybe it is *your* fault! However, I could understand that if it was, then at least we could have the peace Jojo was looking for.

It was nothing for me really, I shouldn't complain. Joanne had to track her cycles and go for ultrasounds every couple of days, and then have a dye test to see if "all the plumbing" was clear.

"Everything is fine," the doctor told her. Turns out she was ovulating later in her cycle, so our timing was off. The days we *thought* were the best days for romance were not at all! Would you believe, a couple of weeks later, she was pregnant!

"Eleven years," Jojo laughed. "I was convinced it was my fault. All I needed was a doctor to tell me nothing was wrong with me!"

It was funny because she knew it right away. She was craving peanut butter all the time and feeling light-headed. We were going to her Aunt's birthday party and the venue was right next to a McDonalds. My wife *never* goes to McDonalds.

"I want some fries," she said.

"Really?" I said incredulously. Since we were early for the party, we went in to get a small fries, which she then proceeded to inhale!

"I'm beginning to think I'm pregnant," she joked.

A few days later, Joanne told me to sit down, that she needed to talk to me.

"All right what's up?" I asked.

"I AM pregnant!" she said, grinning from ear to ear. "I have to confirm it with the doctor, but I'm 99% positive I am."

How can I describe how I felt? I was forty two years old! Joanne was thirty-five. I had never thought I would find the love of my life never mind have a child too. I'm not ashamed to say I had tears in my eyes.

Everyone kept saying she was having a boy, you know all those silly superstitions about the way she was carrying and stuff. I did want a boy. What man doesn't want a son? Joanne really wanted a girl, she kept referring to the baby as 'he' and 'Bruno Jr' because she didn't want to jinx it. I know my father wanted it to be a boy. My sister had a boy, but he was not a DeLuca.

Dad always used to say:

"When I have a grandson with my name, then I can die."

"Well, I hope it's not a boy," Joanne said later. "I don't want to be responsible for him dropping dead! I *certainly* don't want to name my son Johnny!"

The thing about Jojo though, she is always looking for ways to compromise and make everyone happy, so one day she says to me:

"What would you think about naming the baby Jonatan? In Polish it would be Jan for short, it's the same as John. We can use my father's name as his middle name and put it in Italian, out of respect for that part of his heritage too."

I thought it was a fantastic idea!

"Babe, this is why I love you!" I said. "I really appreciate this."

We told my family and we thought that they'd be happy. Sadly, this was not the case. One day when I was visiting my parents, my father let me know what he really thought.

"I'm not happy. It's not right that the baby be named Jan. He is not Polish. This is Canada, he should be John."

"Jojo doesn't want John. She is trying to make everyone happy this way."

"Jan is just stupid. It's disrespectful to me!"

I wasn't surprised by it. Things had been going too well for it to last. This was just my father wanting things his own way again. Not even my unborn child was safe. I suppose I should have kept my mouth shut, but I was upset. I told Joanne about it, and she almost lost her shit.

"You know what's disrespectful? Him not saying this to my face!" she seethed. "All this Canada stuff is bull-shit! If we were to name him Giovanni he'd be over the moon!"

"So what do you want to do?"

"I wish I could change it now, but I'm used to it. His name will be Jonatan Andreas, I've already told my father and *he* is happy with it. But I promise you this, if this child is a girl, there will be no compromises on a second child."

Joanne's pregnancy went pretty well. She described it as a walk in the park. All was ready to go when Bruno Jr decided to do a back flip two weeks before the due date. Jojo was in a lot of pain, she left work early and could hardly move.

"I think you better go see the doctor," I said.

"I'm going tomorrow," she said.

The doctor took one look at her and said she was to go see her at the hospital first thing the next morning.

"I was hooked up to the monitor for an hour," Jojo said. "I didn't think anything was wrong, I just thought it was normal discomfort from having a person inside me ready to come out. I sat there doing my knitting and the nurses were popping in from time to time, checking the print-outs.

"The doctor came in and she says, 'Do you know that you're in labor?' I said 'What? Really?'"

I got a hysterical call from Joanne. She had been trying to reach me for a couple of hours and I was the last person she got a hold of!

"The baby is upside down and the doctor says my blood pressure is high and he's got to come out and I need a C-section and I'm so scared and you're not here and everyone else is here and it's going to be at three and it's already one and are you going to make it?!"

"Calm down Babe!" I said. "I'll be there!"

So the walk in the park ended with a pretty difficult delivery by C-section.

"It's a girl", the doctor announced calmly while unwrapping my poor 'Bruno junior' from loops and loops of umbilical cord.

"Why isn't she crying? Why isn't she crying?!" Jojo bawled hysterically through a drug induced fog.

It was a super tense moment waiting for that first cry. Looking back at the video I took is actually more traumatic to me than how I felt at the time. All those people huddled around my baby with tubes and bags and the urgency with which they worked. Then suddenly, that little mewl, then a big breath and crying started. You could see her skin turn from blue to bright red. Wow!

"A girl, a girl!" Joanne mumbled with relief.

The baby was wrapped up and I held her next to Jojo's face so she could say hello to her at last. I felt bad, but I didn't want to stick around for the sewing up part. The nurses pretty much shooed me out anyway.

I thought my heart would burst as I walked down the hall with that little bundle in my arms. As I approached my family all crowded around the lounge entrance, I could see how tense they all were waiting to hear the news and see the baby.

"It's a girl!" I said.

You would have thought I had said we'd all won the lottery.

The scream that came out of Joanne's mother and sister nearly scared the shit out of me! It certainly pissed off the ladies at the nursing station.

"Excuse me, I know you're very excited but could you please keep it down?" the charge nurse said. "There are babies and very tired mothers in here!"

"Sorry, sorry," my mother-in-law blubbered through tears of joy. "A girl! A girl!"

Apparently baby girls are big deals in my wife's family. I don't know why! They have so many! You'd think they'd want a boy more!

My father was happy, but I could tell by his wry smile that he was disappointed. I didn't care! Nothing was going to bring me down this day.

After a year or so had passed, there was no sign of another Bruno Jr. We were happy with Abigail though. I finally had the family I always wanted. More children would have been wonderful, but we both were so grateful for the gift of our little girl.

I feel in my life, that I have always needed to be in charge. Other individuals always look at other people what they are doing. When they should just be focused on their lives. For example, that person took an extra five minutes on break. Are you going to talk to her? Why, for five minutes? So they will do the same thing, people cannot live their lives. So then I will say you can take an extra five minutes too, but you cannot leave until your work is done. The person that took the extra five minutes, it maybe happens once in a while or even two times a week. For ten minutes in a week, does that really make a difference in the week?

I truly believe people in general cause problems because they are not happy within their own lives. If you are not happy in the situation you are in, do what will make you happy. Sometimes it may take risk, but it is worth it if you will be happy at end of it all. It's funny, my kids are still very young but I always tell them you can do whatever you want in your life. With my father, that was not the case. He wanted me to do what he wanted.

When I applied for the position of Bakery Manager and I told my dad, right away he was against it, saying you're not going to be able to handle it because it is a supermarket. I told him I did not apply for Store Manager, I applied for Bakery Manager. What it was he thought I couldn't handle, I don't know! My father never was encouraging in my life for anything. I know what the problem was, he was jealous. That word again, but it is true! He did not want me to do better than him. I'm not trying to do better than him. I just like being my *own* boss. He didn't understand what I wanted from La Roma Bakery. It's not just being the boss, but I love making desserts and cakes. I did not want to be around this man because he was not good to me.

I wanted to move up in the company though. I wanted to be a Bakery Merchandiser. They kept on saying it will happen, but it never did. They wanted me stay as a bakery manager because I was very good at it. I understand it, but I don't agree with it. I had many ideas that I could have helped the bakery departments make more money and also have better departments. I remember one of my merchandisers, she did not know anything about the bakery, but she got the position. Isn't that odd? She always came to ME for help! She did not even understand bakery equipment! I guess when you do "special favors", you get the support you want. I knew that I was not going anywhere with this company, so I had to make a decision. Do I stay, or move on to a new opportunity? So, I decided to start looking elsewhere.

*You shall eat the fruit of the labor of your hands; you shall be happy, and it shall be well with you.*

*Psalm 128: 2*

I sure did work a lot in those days. There were days that Joanne was very lonely. Often we would fight about how little time I was spending at home.

I think a lesser woman would have left me, but not my Jojo. To make up for me not being at home, she would often come and visit me at my second job at La Giardino Bakery and Grocery. I can still picture her sitting on a muffin pail with her little baby belly sticking out!

It was unfortunate that La Giardino was so close to my father's house. He knew I was working there and often made a point to visit and criticize my work. It was very annoying having him in the back room looking over my shoulder and telling me that he could do whatever I was doing better.

"I saw the Amaretti you did the other day," he said once. "They weren't so good. I can't understand why Gina put them out."

"What the hell are you talking about?!" I said.

"Gina told me she was not happy, but that she had no choice but to use them."

"Whatever," I said. I did not feel like arguing that day.

The next time I was in, Gina approached me to tell me that my dad had been there.

"I know," I said. "Apparently my Amaretti are no good."

"Bruno, you make fantastic cookies," she said after I told her what my dad had said. "I don't know why your father would say that."

Sam, a good friend of mine that was working on the side with me at La Giardino told me that there was an opportunity at Sunflower Foods where he worked as a sales person. I said "sales?" I'd never worked in sales before so I asked him what they sold. Apparently, it was bakery supplies. He told me they are looking for a sales guy with a bakery background. Well, that would be just perfect for me. I asked him what the pay is like. This is going back eight years ago. Sam said that they would probably offer you fifty grand a year and there is a bonus for every month if you hit your budget. Plus a company car, gas card and expense account. That sounded pretty good to me. He told me get myself a resume. So I got my resume done and he brought it in. He told me eight guys including me had applied for this position.

When I applied for this job, my father tried to talk me out of it.

"I don't think you can handle it. It's a big position and you've never done it before. It's a lot of responsibility."

"I want the challenge," I said. "Don't you see that I have to push myself to be better in my life once again?"

"You don't know what you're getting into." He was never positive with any career move I made. I never had his blessing for anything. Whenever I tried something new, he would always say: I did it first. Not saying he didn't, but it is always about him. He just cannot be happy for me. What I see, is that he is jealous of his own son. I hope my son is happy in life and does better than his dad. I would do everything for my kids. I thank God for my kids and pray for the best for them.

I remember telling one of my customers that I pray for my kids and their generations going forward. She tells me I have never heard of anyone doing that. My only response to that was "really?" I could not believe it, are people that focused only on their own lives? I don't understand that, having kids.

Four months later I was thinking I wasn't going to get the job, but I finally got a call, and I was ready. My first interview was with the branch manager. I thought that it went well. He was very impressed with my background and also all my accomplishments. He told me that he would get back to me to have an interview with his sale manager. I told him I would be looking forward to meeting with him. I was so excited that I might have a chance to get this job. I knew I was qualified, I know I didn't have the fancy diplomas but I understood the bakery business. I also knew a lot of people in the bakery world.

Well, the day came when I had an interview with the sales manager, Al. We had a very similar background. He also had been a bakery manager. So we talked quite bit about our positions. It was a very nice conversation and then we went into the interview. Al was pretty impressed with my history. He asked what I would do to increase sales. I replied that someone who has worked with the products and knows them well is the best person to sell them. Clients would not just get a sales rep with me, they would also get a technical advisor and a business coach. I wasn't shy about letting him know how much I wanted the opportunity. I guess he saw that I was ambitious.

When the interview came to an end, he told me that it was between me and one other candidate. After two weeks I got called back to come in and hear their offer.

I was so excited to tell my family.

"You don't know what you're getting into," my dad said. "You think everything is so easy, but it's not easy."

"Wow," Jojo said. "Can't you just say that you're happy for him?"

"I am happy for him!" he retorted. "But at the same time I'm not happy for him. I'm worried about him!"

That's my dad, always being negative.

"At least he worries for you," my wife said later. "Too bad he can't just come out and say he loves you."

"He's not worried about me," I said, "He's worried that I'll make him look bad."

Joanne shrugged, "Well, there is nothing you can do about what he thinks. The best thing you can do now is to do this job and be great at it."

I started in March 2009. My wife was five months pregnant with Abigail at that time and I was worried about having to take some time off for the birth, but that wasn't a problem. I was so happy to get this position because I love helping people grow their business. The first week I was training with Al and it was a lot of fun. We had breakfast together and talked about how I should go about getting customers and enjoying each other's company.

I remember doing some cold calls in the Niagara area and I was confident and nervous at the same time. I thought it would be easy, but it was not as easy as I thought! We did two more cold calls in Mississauga which was part of my territory. We approached Firenze Bakery and one of the owners said:

"Is that you Bruno?"

Of course, I said yes it is me. I introduced Al to Domenic and he said "So, what are you doing now?"

"I'm working for a company called Sunflower Foods."

"I've heard of you guys. Are you in sales now? You're done with being a pastry chef? I heard you were a bakery manager."

"Yes, I was a bakery manager for a while. I wanted to grow within the company, but it would have taken forever, so I decided to make a move," I told him. "Now I am here with Sunflower Foods and it's been good. Anyhow, when are we going to open up an account?"

"I already deal with another company, but because it is you I will open up an account."

"Thanks Dom and if you need any support I am here for you."

"I know! And I will be asking soon!"

My boss was shocked that we walked into this first account and I knew this owner. We went to do another cold call at Anna's Bakery. The owner was Roberto and after we introduced ourselves he said;

"Didn't you own La Roma Bakery?"

"Yes, I was one of the owners."

He was going on about how big our bakery was and I just responded by being humble. Thank God that things worked out our way.

"Bruno, what was your secret?" Roberto asked.

"Well, there were a few things that we did and also a little luck was on our side." I replied.

"Ha! I know your secret. It was hard work! Can you tell my son that?"

"Yes your dad is right, you need to work at it and you need to want it." I said to his son.

"I'm building this business for my son." Roberto said.

"That is great, but *you* have to want the business too."

He agreed.

"Come by next week and we will open up an account. I don't mind helping happy young people."

Happy YOUNG people?! I laughed to myself. Who me? I was on the wrong side of forty already. I wished I was young again!

This conversation made me think about something my brother said. So many people want to be rich, but maybe only a small percentage of those people will take the action needed to manifest that desire. You can't just sit around and wish to be rich or think about being rich. You need to do something about it, and that will take work. As long as you want it and believe in yourself, you will see those things fall into place.

We went by La Roma Bakery and met with Marco, one of the owners that we sold the bakery to. I told him that I could help him with a lot of things including recipes if he needed anything. He kind of brushed me off, but I never gave up. I kept on going back over and over again.

One day when I was there he asked if I would like an espresso. Of course, I never say no to an espresso! We got to talking and he says to me;

"Bruno, you guys sold me a gold mine of a business."

"I know," I smiled sadly, "But, I am happy you are doing well."

Within our conversation it sounded like life was very good for him. Being there, for me, it brought back memories. Good and bad memories; the success of La Roma Bakery and the bad at not being on the same page with my father.

Marco had renovated the bakery and it looked great. Anyhow, he says, let's open up account and take it slow. I knew that this bakery was very busy, and that this would be a good account for Sunflower Foods.

It wasn't all so easy in the beginning. I remember coming home and telling my wife that I had a headache that had been going on for weeks. I was so stressed out because I wasn't used to this kind of job. The computer work and reporting was all foreign to me. For a while I thought I may have made a mistake.

My wife said, "No, you didn't. You just need some help."

She found a computer course for me to take to acquire some basic skills.

"The rest is easy," she said. "I don't know a heck of a lot about computers and I use the programs at the hospital just fine. Sunflower probably has all their spread sheets made out. You just have to learn the programs that they use and most of them are pretty user friendly. And remember, I am here to help you."

I do love the job. It was a lot of fun because of my background. Well, three months into the job and I was doing well. I opened up eighteen accounts. I was so pleased with myself.

I thought that I had finally found something that I would enjoy doing for the rest of my life. I do love helping people and giving them ideas and technical support. But in the back of my head, I missed La Roma Bakery. I loved my bakery! People always ask me why I don't go back in business. I would love to, but not to start over. I'm just too old!

When I was bakery manager, the produce manager always asked me to open up a business with him. He said we would do so well, I told him that I didn't disagree. But at that time I was still very angry with what happened at La Roma Bakery. I just did not want anything to do with business.

One of the things I love doing at Sunflower is working in the labs. It's where we get the products we sell and test them out by making different things. Also, making things in the bakeries when I am providing technical support. Needless to say, I do get to bring a lot of sweets home with me. I was always bringing stuff to my family at dinner time.

One day, Joanne lost her patience with me. I brought some Easter bread over. My dad right away had to criticize. It was not yellow enough. Why was the taste not quite right? Well, it is good, but my way of doing it is better.

"Why do you keep providing him with the ammunition to hurt you!" she said.

"What do you mean?" I said.

"You keep bringing stuff over to him and he rips it apart, you may as well hand your heart over to him on a platter and let him stab it," she said.

"I just want him to see that I can still do good stuff."

"Why do you care? *You* know you do good stuff! You don't need *his* approval! You're never going to get it anyway."

That was really hard to swallow. I never had thought of it that way before, but she was right. There was a part of me that still wanted to hear my dad say "Good job, son." I had not let it go, and every time he put me down it was another kick in the chest. So, I stopped bringing sweets over.

As time went by, my dad remarked;

"How come you never bring anything over anymore?"

"Why should he?" my wife piped up, "All you do is tear it up anyway."

"Well, I'm just saying the truth," he said. "If something is good I will say so."

My wife just shrugged. She told me later, "You will never get satisfaction from him. It is hard I know, it was the hardest lesson I had to learn in my life too. But all that truly matters is how you feel about yourself, then you won't need his approval and you will be happy."

My wife's family gets the benefit of all the sweets now. If I asked them what they thought about a particular product compared to something else, or to provide me with feedback, they are more than happy to be honest. But my mother-in-law can never say anything bad. She loves the sweets too much!

Joanne is a great support, in that she doesn't always say what I want to hear. Sometimes I resist really hard what she says, but she understands that, because she went through that resistance too. For instance, I was in one of my down moods, talking about all the things that could have been, she dropped this bomb on me:

"Bruno, why didn't you just leave?"

It caught me off guard.

"Because I couldn't."

"Yes, you could've," she said.

"My family would have disowned me! They would have lost everything and they would have blamed me."

"So? You made your own reasons for staying, but no one forced you to. You could have left. It would have been hard, very hard. But your life was hard anyway, you have to accept your responsibility for what happened to you."

"How can you of all people say that me!" I was really mad now.

"Because I know this is the hardest lesson to learn!" she said. "Most of our life's troubles are our *own* fault! I'm not saying that what your dad did to you was right or justified. What my ex-husband did to me was not right and not fair either, but no one *forced* me to marry him! I knew something was not right and that I was not truly happy and I married him anyway. Then I put up with his shit all those years when I could have left sooner and told myself I was staying with him because it was the right thing to do.

"*You* know how *stupid* I felt when I finally left him! It was you who told me to think about it as part of my life's journey and to accept it. I will never get satisfaction from my ex, ever. But I don't need it because I've forgiven myself for being taken advantage of, and so now I can forgive him for taking advantage of me."

Ah, wives, what would we do without them to knock some sense into us once and a while?

After getting question after question about when the next baby was coming, Joanne was beginning to think that there wasn't going to *be* another baby.

"Would you be okay with that?" Jojo asked me.

"I'm okay," I assured her. "I'm worried that you're disappointed."

"I waited so long for Abigail," she said, "I can't be disappointed. I just think we should let everyone else know so they can get off our case. Your family's not the problem really, it's mine. My mom is relentless."

So Jojo let everyone know not to expect any new DeLucas.

Two weeks later, Joanne was huddled up on the couch in a blanket, complaining about how she felt like shit as I handed her some gravol tablets.

"Well, you can't be pregnant," I said. She looked up at me.

"Oh yes, I can!" she snapped. "In fact, I'm pretty sure I am. Last night, I couldn't even rock Abigail to sleep in the rocking chair without feeling like I was going to toss my cookies!"

She had a test left over from Abigail so she tried it out the next morning. She insisted it was positive but I couldn't see anything!

"It's there!" she insisted. "Look, there is a really faint blue line. This is a cheap test and it's old. I'll make an appointment with the doctor."

Well, the pee-test at the doctor didn't show anything either.

"I'm telling you, I'm pregnant." Jojo insisted. "It's just really early and I haven't missed a period yet."

"Okay, I'll give you an order for the blood test and that will clear everything up," the doctor said. I'm pretty sure she was just humoring her. I was beginning to think that my wife was going nuts! Yet, in the end she was right! The blood test came back positive. Talk about a woman who knows her own body!

So there it began, and it didn't get any better for poor Jojo. She was so sick the first few months, then she got a terrible rash all over her body that made her itch like crazy. She had to sit on a pillow all the time because her butt was so sore.

"I bet this is a boy," she complained. "It's like I'm having an allergic reaction to him!"

Sure enough, the ultra-sound confirmed it. I hate it when she's right! I had a feeling it was a boy too, and I was so excited!

About half way through the pregnancy, Joanne's skin began to clear up, but then she started getting horrible break outs on her face.

She was so embarrassed to go out in public. And tired! She was so tired all the time. I didn't think a person could sleep so much. Bruno Jr had taken everything she had. At the end, Joanne was just big belly with sticks for arms and legs.

When we began discussing names for him, Joanne kept her promise. She would not budge on the name.

"Jonathan can be his middle name," she said. "That's all the compromise I'm willing to give."

"You have to be the better person," I said. "I don't mind naming him John."

Well, I guess that was the wrong thing to say because Joanne blew up like a damn volcano!

"It's not about being the better damn person!" she yelled. "You are the one all these years telling me how badly he treated you! And you want me to name my child after *him*?

"If you two were close, genuinely *close,* you would have no argument from me! But you're not close at all! He's trying to claim your son, don't you see? This is *your* son, not *his* son. He had his chance with sons and he blew it! This is *your* chance!"

I suppose I was deceiving myself. I wanted to pretend that I had a good relationship with my dad. I guess I was hoping that naming my boy after him would bring us closer, but in my heart I knew it wouldn't. My father simply *expected* the child to be named after him, like it was his right! I could see Joanne's point. I know she was right. It really hurt though, it brought back a lot of painful memories, and the more I thought about it, the more I was resigned to the fact that *I* would be the one to name my son.

We threw around a few names and had it narrowed down to Michael, Steve and Dylan when the day of the birth came. Joanne had decided to go with a planned C-section because she would have had to go far out of town and be treated like a severe case if she hadn't.

"How about Bruno?" I asked as she was putting on the hospital gown.

"That's fine with me," she paused thoughtfully. "But you better promise me not to call him Junior! I hate Junior!"

*Give, and it will be given to you; good measure, pressed down, shaken together, running over, will be put into your lap. For the measure you give will be the measure you get back.*

*Luke 6: 38*

One day I did cold call at a bakery called The Big Bagel. A young man named Erik came out to meet me and I told him about my back ground. He told me his family had just taken over the bakery. Like the sign said, they had big bagels and also, amazing rye bread.

I became very close to Erik and in time we became good friends. I guess he reminded me a bit of me at that age. Also they are a Polish family and my Jojo is part Polish. I told Erik that when I was younger I had a Polish girlfriend and she was a sweetheart. At the time I loved her, but made the mistake of listening to my friends. Young and stupid.

Like me, he had a lot a beautiful girlfriends. As time went by, he met a girl called Ivony at work, someone that they hired. She was pretty, but not a model if you know what I mean. But, to make a long story short, he fell in love with her. Why? Because love is more than just looks. She was a hard worker and knew the value of what they were putting into the business. She is wonderful person inside and out.

One day at the bakery he proposed to her and she said yes. I gave them a big hug and congratulated them both. They asked me if I can do them a favor and make their wedding cake.

"No problem. It is as good as done"

The day of the wedding was beautiful, it was on their property in Owen Sound. They had two acres of property with an outdoor hall. The wedding was amazing and the food was amazing.

That's one of the biggest rewards of the line of work I am in, I get to meet so many different kinds of people and form good, genuine relationships with some of them. I was really enjoying my job. It was so much fun and I had a lot of support from my sales manager.

One day, I got phone call from this woman. Her name was Marta and she was asking for samples for her sons.

"My boys are going to open up a bakery," she said. "Right now we are working from our basement."

I asked for the address and I brought them some samples. She was so happy that I was bringing the samples. They had gone to other suppliers but they had basically brushed them off and said they were too small.

"I can help the boys where they need it," I said. "I am a pastry chef and also I had my own business for fourteen years."

"That is great because we've never be in business before and we need all the help we can get."

I didn't know it at the time, but this small act was a big deal to the Viscardi family, and it was the start of a very long and rewarding relationship with them.

I arrived at the house, and she was so welcoming. She offered me a coffee and food. They were Italians that is the norm within our culture. But really, Marta is a sweetheart.

When the boys came out, I was shocked. Why? They were identical twins! What are the chances of coming across twins in the industry?

They would become a pain in my ass! Why? They do not talk! To get a word out of them is like pulling teeth! It was hard to see what they envisioned in the future for their bakery.

I told Peter and Paul a little bit about my background and how my father and I did not get along. They did have a lot to say about their dad. They said he was not the easiest guy to work with. My advice was not to have their dad as a partner, but that was mostly based on what had happened to me.

Poor Anthony, I didn't give him enough credit. But I hadn't met him yet and I didn't know him. He *was* difficult to work with at times but everything he did was for his boys and he was in it to help them out. The boys complained a lot about him, but the man worked *hard*.

I offered them all kinds of recipes because I was not sure where they were going in their bakery. There was time I wanted to kill them both, but again, Marta was such a sweetheart so I stuck with them for her. These kids were just the worst at seeing the big picture. They only wanted to do custom cakes, and I kept trying to tell them that there was no way to build a business just on that. Not to say that they weren't talented, because the work that they did was wonderful. These boys were truly gifted.

I think they loved me, but I bothered them because I said what was true and not what they wanted to hear. There was more than one time I lost my temper. But, you know, they were always respectful, even to this day. Yes, these are the nicest boys you will ever meet. Their parents did a great job with them and their oldest son Adam.

Ah, Adam! All serious and all business! You could have sworn he and his brothers were triplets, except he was a big beast compared to them. He just had this rough look about him, he shaved his head and was into body building. I was not too fond of him, at first.

"Marta, did Adam just get out of jail?" I said after I had met him.

"What is wrong with Adam? He is a good guy!" she leapt right to his defense.

"He looks a criminal, he has the look of death!" I said.

"Come on, Bruno, that is not nice!"

"But it is true, would you want to do business with that guy? Best he stays in the office," I said.

Knowing Adam today all these years later, we are like best friends. I am the kind guy that I do not have best friends but I can put him on my list as a good one. I wish I can say the same thing about the other two, but it is hard to get close to them when they are *mute!*

Two years later, the Viscardis had out-grown their shop in the basement, the boys started looking for a real store. They had searched out a place in Etobicoke, they told me all about it. They wanted to add cupcakes because it was trendy at the time.

"What do *you* want to do?" I asked.

"What would *you* do?" they replied. I guess they really trusted in my judgement.

"Because of the size of the shop, I would do pastries, cookies, breakfast items and cakes. Plus the cupcakes and custom cakes."

The store was called La Napolitano Bakery.

Adam was a real asset to the store. He was all business. Smart kid! He was always asking questions about the industry. Which is the way it should be, if you want to learn! I met with them quite often to help them get the store going.

I also began getting to know Anthony better and I liked him very much. The man had balls. He was a very confident gentleman. We used to talk all the time; he had big dreams for his boys.

I could see where the boys were having difficulty with him though. They were young men coming into their own and they didn't want to be told what to do by their dad. He was old-school and really set in his ways, even if those ways weren't always right. He did remind me of my father a bit, except for the fact this was a man that loved his kids and he did the best that he could for them.

Anyhow let's move on, I came across an account called India Sweets and I was trying for six months to get into this account. For the life of me I was not going anywhere fast. One day the pastry chef, Eman finally came out and reached out to me.

"You've been coming every week for at least six months, you don't give up," he said.

"All I want is a chance to introduce our products and if you need any technical support, I can help. I am a pastry chef as well."

He told me what he was looking for and if Sunflower had the better product and price, he would buy. That night I did pricing for him. The next day he looked at it and said it looked good. He said lets open up an account and I will give you my first order for next week.

It is funny when I mention that I am a pastry chef that other pastry chefs get their guard up. All I say is that if you need any help, I am here for you. I want us to be friends and I am not here to compete with you. They seem to think that as pastry chefs they already know everything. No matter what you know, you can always learn something.

After a while Eman and I became very good friends. He trusted me, but he also tested me. He'd ask me for different recipes and I offered them willingly. Mind you, he already had all these recipes. Pastry chefs are funny, they have all these recipes, but they will ask for the same recipe just to see the difference. That is fine with me, but there are times where they do not have that recipe and they need your help. I really like Eman, he is a good guy and a great pastry chef. I think how lucky I was to have a job like this. Even though everything that happened to me in my life, I am so grateful.

Then one day a new bakery opened up in Mississauga and a fellow sales guy told me he knew them. So I approached the bakery and mentioned his name and they said yes we dealt with him for five years. I told them that I would be their new sale guy and I am a pastry chef. The owner put up her guard right away. She said she was a certified pastry chef for thirty five years.

"Also my son went to college and is a pastry chef as well."

I just said what I always say,

"If you need any help I will be more than happy to help you."

"We are fine, but thank you," she said.

Both Iva and Philip are very talented people. I could tell right away by the quality of work I saw in the store that day. I understand that people need to get to know you and trust you before anything happens. As time went by I was being supportive in answering any questions they had.

Iva and her husband Don asked me if I would do a presentation for them on cakes and pastries. So the following week I did the presentation and they were impressed.

"You really are a Master," she said.

"Listen" I said, "I am just here to help you."

As time went by we became friends as well. I brought my family to the store at Christmas time and they gave me a gift. As I opened up the gift, my eyes could not believe what I saw. Can you believe they gave me five-hundred dollars in cash?!

"I can't accept this!" I told then. "What I did for you I would do for any of my clients. I enjoy helping people succeed."

"You better take it!" Don insisted in his thick Greek accent. "If you do not it is an insult to me!"

Far be it from me to insult someone! I must have said thank you a thousand times.

When we had our Christmas lunch at Sunflower Foods, I told my boss what happened and he was shocked that they gave me so much. He made it a point to tell the whole sale team and said that is customer service. My branch manager was very impressed and came to shake my hand. It was all nice, but at the end of the day I was just doing my job, it is just because I care.

After five years with the company, they decided to give me a new territory to build up. It was probably the worst territory in Ontario. But I took it as a challenge. This is the number I had: $1,525.000 for the year. My budget was $1,620.000 for the year. For the year I did $1,575.000. I was off quite a bit, that year I had surgery on my eye and we had lost one sales guy on our team. Three of us had to take care of that territory. The following year my budget was $1,675.000 for the year. I hit my budget and went beyond at $1,900.000. I was on fire! I had something to prove! I was very proud of myself for what I accomplished. You've got to remember you have to keep in account on where the economy is in that year. Every year is different. Also they gave me the worst territory.

I came across some new accounts, where I also gave them some support. One of the accounts was Rosa Bakery. Sandy wanted to know how to make shortbread cookies and to give her different ideas to grow the business. I love helping people and making them be successful. This account are fantastic people and good friends of mine.

I talked to my dad a lot about Sunflower because he was working at one of my accounts and he placed his orders with me. My father was impressed that the company was as big as it was. The company is worldwide and is a two billion dollar company. I was saying how much I love the job at Sunflower because of the quality of the product and the technical support that I can give my accounts.

"I know you, you just want to show off," he said.

"What are you talking about? It's my job to help my customers."

"You don't have to tell them everything. You just want to look like a big shot."

That could have been the start of a *really* bad argument, but my wife kicked me a few times under the table, and I kept my peace.

"You have to remember, what he says to you is really about him and not you. Understand?" she said later. "*He* is the show-off, so he automatically assumes that is what you are doing, not that you genuinely want to help people."

I tried not to let it bother me, but it did. I guess I still just want to hear him say something positive.

I was opening all kinds of new accounts. I came across an account that was already opened. I went to meet them for the first time. The father did not say boo to me, his daughter talked to me, also his wife talked to me and then there is Ralph. He is the pastry chef and he is good. He always does different deserts and I love that in a bakery.

I love Ralph and his mother Stephanie. She was always good to me and whenever anything bad happened. By bad, I mean with her husband. He was always late paying, and it was hard to get him to pay up.

Anyway, there was a guy called Joe who worked there who talked very badly about God. He was saying things like if I ever see him, I will tell him to go f-himself and things along those lines. I asked Stephanie what was wrong with this guy. Stephanie said I know, you should not say things like that about God, but I also heard he tried to burn down a church.

Once I was there again and he was rambling on about God again and I could not take it anymore.

"Buddy, what do you have against God?" I asked.

"He took my wife!"

"I am sorry about your wife, but the world took your wife, not the Lord. You should not talk about God that way."

"I don't care about God or your excuses," he said. "When I finally see him, I am going to punch him."

Then I lost it!

"When you meet your Maker," I said, "You won't be *able* to say a word. You think of Him in human form, but He is not. You think He is like you? He is *nothing* like you."

"I don't care."

"You know there is still hope for you, as long as you ask for forgiveness and you are sincere about it. You will go to heaven!"

He said "Never!"

"One day, you when you face Him, you will remember this conversation. You made your own bed. That's all I have to say."

He was angry with me because I love God and also what I told him. He never talked to me again. I prayed for him because he is lost.

"Stephanie," I said. "I don't want to be judgmental. This situation is about our religion. Why should we keep quiet when people insult us because of Him? We have to be more like Him and be good people and help people where we can. Can you imagine if we were all good to each other, how this great this world would be?"

"You are a good man, Bruno," she said. "I've never heard anyone talk about God like you do."

Then there is Milan Bakery, they are all very respectful. There is John and I love his personality. He says it the way it is. I would like to thank him because every time I come there he makes me laugh. We need more people like that in the world. Then there is Ozzie, we always talk about the Leafs or the national Italian soccer team. Sometimes it seems fixed. Everyone knows the mob is involved and it's all about the money. I think it is sad if that is the case, you don't look forward to the winner because you do not know if it is all fixed.

Then we have the two Sams, Sam senior and Sam junior. Sam Jr is always singing, which is nice to see because it says that he is happy. Sam senior, is just Sam. Nice guy and he offers you whatever he brings from the market. The last son, Mario. He is a man that is firm, but he is also a comedian. Which shocked me, but he only goes on stage a few times a year.

The company asked me if I would take over an account called Salvatore Bakery. I did not want to, because La Prima had been right around the corner from there. Once again, La Prima Bakery did very well, and I did not feel right being there with Salvatore so close. My father was told not to come there, but he does not listen to anyone.

Well, I came to the bakery to get an order and met the owner, Jim. This man was a beast. The guy was a monster! I told him that I was his new sales rep from Sunflower Foods. He said that is fine. I went there every week and he gave me nice orders. I also met with Jim's dad, James. You know what just a real nice guy is. I actually enjoyed his company. I've been going there for three years now. Jim and his father are just great guys. I hook up with Chris, their old sale rep from Sunflower Foods. We both say this it just such a great account because we have so much fun.

One day, I guess Jim took a real good look at my business card and noticed my last name. He calls me over for a little chat.

"Bruno are you one of the owners of La Prima Bakery and also you owned La Roma Bakery."

It wasn't a question, he knew who I was! Jim was very upset with my dad back in the day because he was in front of Salvatore giving out flyers for La Prima. I can understand that! Seems like a pretty tacky thing to do.

"Yeah, but those days are done," I said. "I know you weren't too happy with my dad when La Prima was here, but look, you are still here and doing well."

Jim could easily tell me to take a hike and not to come back, but he didn't! I have a lot of respect for this family. They kept buying from me, which I am grateful for! Once again, a great family!

*"As life goes on, you have to bond with people. Don't be afraid to show your love, because bonding is a beautiful thing."*
                                                        Anthony Viscardi

The Viscardis started talking about moving La Napolitano to a bigger location. They spent four years in that first small store. I told them that it would always be difficult for there to be any real profit in that tiny place. They all agreed! So they started looking. They finally found a location.

They wanted me to see the place and I loved it. There is a lot traffic through there and also a better lease because it is in a commercial building. The store frontage is great, easily seen from the road and it is very busy. I said your dad is great in that because he was in sales, he'll know what to do to get people here. There were other sales guys saying you won't do well here and I told Adam not to listen to them. If you advertise, you can't go wrong.

At the beginning it was tough for them, running two shops. Adam one day called and said I need your help. I got together with him and I advised them what they should do. They did take my advice and after six months the new location was busy enough for them to shut down the old location. I was telling them it takes time to grow your business, but it will come. They didn't have much money, but they would buy pizza every Saturday for their staff. I thought that was nice of them. Once again a great bunch of guys! I think personally they were a little too easy going with their staff.

A couple of times I came in the bakery showed them a few things they should be doing. I showed them how to do almond cookies, shortbread cookies (the ones you cut and drop with a bag), gave all kinds of different ideas with the puff pastries, to do zeppole, gave them different cake and cheesecake ideas, loaf cakes, etc. I so proud of them because sales are doing well.

Then I got the phone call. Adam called early one morning.

"What's up Adam?"

"My-my father just died this morning," came the dead pan response.

"What? Oh my God, Adam I'm so sorry! What happened?" I asked.

"He had a heart attack in his sleep," he said.

"Is there anything I can do?"

"Can you go by the bakery and just guide everybody through what has to be done?" Adam asked. "I can't do it!"

I drove right to La Napolitano. They were all in shock! I knew that they just hired a new decorator. I set her to doing custom cake work because a cake or two had to get done that day. Connie worked on other cake orders. Michael was doing his work load, pastries and cakes. Lana had to leave her work area a few times to go and cry.

This broke my heart because, Anthony was a rock to his boys. I started crying many times as well, I just could not help myself. For the boys though, there was no time to grieve. They had a business to run.

I love these guys, because they still take care of their customers. I saw what they went through, Paul and Peter heart broken, Adam showing no emotion. It was killing me because they loved him so much, they let him do whatever he wanted. Whether he was right or wrong and that is true love towards your father. Those guys didn't know what do, but I was there as friend and just show them that I love them.

Whatever support I gave came from my heart. I do it just to do it! I love this industry and these men. I have the highest respect for them. If life had gone as it should have, I would probably have had kids this age by now. I treat them like they *are* my kids, yes sometimes I bust their asses, because I care. They know what I am talking about. The bakery went through a lot of changes for the better. It was not smooth sailing, but they got through it. They are now at serious note and they are organized. They know what they need to do to reach their goals.

It is funny one of the twins got married back a couple years ago and I was invited to the wedding. The day of the wedding my son was very sick and I could not go. I really wanted to go but it wasn't going to happen. Also, they invited me out for a company day at the baseball game, and I couldn't go because I got sick!

Recently I was invited to Peter and Angela's engagement. I had the invitation for about a month and a week prior from the engagement party, what do I get? Strep throat! Four days I couldn't sleep or eat because of my ears popping. It was difficult to drink water and I was in so much pain. I decided to call La Napolitano to tell Peter that I wouldn't be coming to the engagement. Marta answered the phone.

"Marta, I am so sick and you know what it is?"

She catches her breath and says, "What is it?"

"You have a curse on me!"

"Curse? What curse? What are you talking about?"

"The Napolitano curse!" I laughed. "First with Paul's wedding and now with Peter's engagement. When it comes to the wedding, do not tell me the date. Just tell me three days before the wedding so I can be there!"

She was laughing! "Bruno, you should go to the doctor's and get something for that, okay?"

"You know what? As soon as I get off the phone I will go to a walk in clinic." So I did! They gave me penicillin and soon as I took the first pill, I started feeling better. I called them the next day to let them know I would be coming to the engagement, so the curse is done!

*Likewise the Spirit helps us in our weakness; for we do not know how to pray as we ought, but the Spirit himself intercedes for us with sighs too deep for words. And he who searches the hearts of men knows what is in the mind of the Spirit, because the Spirit intercedes for the saints according to the will of God.*

*We know that in everything God works for good with those who love him, who are called according to his purpose.*

*Romans 8: 26-28*

Being a type I Diabetic has caused lots of problems for me over the years. More than once I have had to go to the hospital. Most of the time it was not my fault, I got the flu or some kind of stomach bug and I had to be admitted to stabilize my blood sugar and be hydrated. There was a time though, when I was not watching my blood sugar properly. I was "cheating" on my insulin, hoping I could bring my sugars down with exercise or some other way. I became so sick, my wife dragged me off to the hospital where I was put in intensive care for a week.

My wife told me the next day, my father was moaning and yelling around the house.

"My son, my son! Lord do not take my son!"

How I wish I could have been there to hear those words, tears came to my eyes when she told me that. Too bad when he came in to see me all he did was yell at me and call me an idiot. Granted, I probably deserved it, but it certainly didn't help matters.

"I don't understand why he just can't tell you how he feels." Joanne said after.

Also on the car ride to the hospital, my dad said to my wife. "I know my son hates me."

Hoping to provoke a discussion, she asked, "Now, why do you think that?"

He just shrugged and said, "I just know."

He just hurt me all my life and he forgot?

If my dad would ever say that to me, "I know that you hate me." What would I like to say to my father?

I know when I got out of the business I *did* hate my dad. If he would have said that to me, I would have told him that I didn't hate him, but that I was very disappointed with him as a man and a father. I was wrong to place my faith and my trust in him with the business. How wrong I was but I still love him. One day we will meet again in the sky above and the truth will be there for both of us. So I will know what went wrong in his life. Oh my father, all I ever wanted from you was to tell me you love me.

I always dream of being his friend and his son, but who knows, life is funny. If he can see what he has done wrong, maybe we can be good friends. My wife tells me to just be his son and ignore the things he says. I try but it is not easy! I cannot thank God for my wife enough! I have a hard time forgetting about it and that is why it is so hard for me to heal. The pain is not as great as it used to be, but it is still there. I try to tell myself to let it go, but it is not easy. I am working on myself to change in a good light. The best way to do that is to have a positive attitude and be positive in my life even when things aren't going so great.

I have heard that most illness are caused by stress or unhappiness within your own life. Sometimes I wonder; just maybe I would not have gotten diabetes if my dad had listened to me. Maybe, I subconsciously wanted to get sick, so he would listen to what I was saying. He did not care unless it was about his life. I used to tell him all the time, it is our money too. My *heart* was too big and he took advantage of it.

Now that I understand things better, I can view everything differently. My father wanted me to be afraid of him. I want my son to respect me, to love me, need me if he needs me and help guide him find his way. I do not want to be sick or angry. I am working trying to forgive my father and remember all the good things in life with him.

I know that when I was born, my dad was so happy. I would like to ask him why he can't be happy with me now. I would say:

I was not born to hurt you, but to be loved by you and to love you just because you are my father. I was born for my dreams, not yours. I was born so you would guide me to be a good human being and to help and respect my fellow brothers and sisters. I was born that my life would have a reason on this planet. I was born to give peace in people's minds, that there is peace within ourselves. I was born to dream and dreams do come true. Don't be afraid to chase your dreams because you should believe in yourself. I was born to bring joy to your life, not hardship. I was born to be your son, not your slave. I was born to tell my son and daughter you were my teacher in this world. A teacher that was not perfect, but believes he was. I was born in this world that I can help you, not be your employee. I am grateful for what you taught me, but why do I feel as if I don't have a real father?

Dad, I want to tell you I have always loved you, so why did you hurt me? Don't you love me? Do you care how I feel? What happened in your life that made you forget about me? I am here waiting for you to tell me that you love me! That you care what I think. That you care what my dreams are. That you cared that one day I wanted a family. Are you glad that I am happy? Does it matter to you? I care for you and I gave my life up for you, did you forget? What can I do to help you? Just because I just love you!

We are all here for a purpose in this world. It can be many things. My dream, Dad, was to help the poor, people in distress, to help anyone who asked and to have my bakery La Roma. Dad, you *can* dream of a better life and it can come true. If you have a dream, then dream and dreams come true. I never left your side because I cared, because I loved you, did you forget? All that I did, I did because I love you. I wanted you by my side and you left me out there alone. I wanted to be by your side, but was I there just for you? You were my superhero once, now I don't know who you are. You were my rock as a child, but you blasted the rock away. When I needed your guidance, you did not care! I had to learn so much on my own. Do you care about the pain I endured? That I loved La Roma Bakery and it killed me to sell it but it was my only way out.

You gave me clothes on my back and food on the table, but you never listened to what I wanted in my life. As if I was not even there! You never listen, but one day we will meet in the sky and it will be all laid out for us. I hope you're ready because He is ready! We will present our cases and let him judge! As we know He is the only who can judge! I can say this to God: I did my best to be a good son and to make you proud of me. Can you say the same? You never hit me, but your words were verbal fists. Instead of hurting my body it destroyed my heart. Don't you understand that when you verbally abuse, you made me feel like garbage? You never wanted to hear about what I needed. I feel like you treated me worse than an animal. You laughed at me as if I was a robot and not a human being with heart and a soul. Did you forget about all that? Or do you still think that you did nothing wrong? What you did to my mother and to us, did you forget? And still, in spite of all this, I can still say that I love you.

*For if you forgive men their trespasses, your heavenly Father also will forgive you; but if you do not forgive men their trespasses, neither will your Father forgive your trespasses.*

*Matthew 6: 14, 15*

I think of my life and I cannot believe that I am still alive after all that. What is wrong with people? The most important thing that your children need is LOVE. You have to support what they decide to do, let them fail, if they must fail, at least they tried. If you don't make mistakes, how can you grow as a human being?

If you have the support, just maybe you might be great in this world! I did well in this world but, not because of my father. It was because of God, I used to go to Him and He helped me chase my dreams and for the time I was under my dad's thumb He helped me cope with that. All I have say is, thank God!

My advice to the human race is that whatever you go through in life, there is still hope! I had nothing and now I have everything. As long as you wake up each morning, you can still dream. What do I mean? You're here and we all have dreams and we all want more and we want to accomplish things. So dream and your dreams will come true, as long as you believe in your dreams. I will be there to tell my children to dream whatever you want. Even if you fail the first time, try again and again and again. If that is what you want, you will have it. All my life my father told me, you can't do that because you have to be a certain person. Always with negative actions, but I am here to tell my kids that they can do anything they want!

I can make a difference in the world, I can share my life to help others, my accomplishments to give hope for others, my kind words to show I care, my advice, my love for others and maybe just a hug and that is all you need.

When you see what you want in your life, focus on it and you will have it. I know because my dreams came true and I am chasing more dreams. My father till this day will not say, "I'm proud of you!" I know why, because that would mean I did better than him in his life. I am not here to compete with him, he is my father not my rival, but he still wants to compete with me. Whatever my kids do with their life, I will be proud of them. As long as they are happy.

When you meet your true love and you start a family, you talk about the gift you are both going to receive. A child! A life! Someone who is actually a *part* of you. Why a parent would verbally abuse their child, be jealous of the child and want to hurt that child is something that I cannot understand. The only thing I can think of is that sometimes, even though a child is a part of you, some people make the mistake of viewing the child as an extension of themselves instead of an individual.

When a kid is small, they are easy to control, they mimic your opinions an actions because they adore you and want to be just like you. But when they grow up, and all of a sudden have their own ideas and plans, suddenly everything changes. I think this is something like what happened to me and my father. I don't know what happened to my dad to make him the way he is. Maybe his father was just like him. Maybe he was worse?

In the end it is about forgiveness. If you can't forgive, then you will always be angry, always be hurt and always be unhappy. I know it is hard, because it doesn't change the wrong that happened to you. I know some people will say, "I can never forgive. Why should I forgive?" But they are viewing it wrong. The person who wronged you is not the one who really needs to be forgiven. They will go on in life as they are whether you forgive them or not. It is you that needs to do the forgiving because it is good for *you*. It makes your soul lighter and it heals you.

It sounds strange, but some people seem to be addicted to their suffering. It is almost like they want to stay angry and miserable.

So I think of it the same way I think about being in business and wanting success. Do you want to be happy? Do you want to be free of this misery? Then you have to take the action needed to achieve that dream. It won't happen overnight, but it will happen. Let go of the past, live for today, plan for the future and be who you are meant to be. Rise above!

God Bless

*Ask, and it will be given you; search, and you will find; knock, and the door will be opened for you.*

*Matthew 7:7*

# Afterword

Just recently, I was sitting in my car at the Rec Centre waiting for my wife to bring the kids out from gymnastics. There was another father there dropping off his son for hockey practice. The boy must have been about thirteen years old.

"Have a good time," he said. He gave his son a big hug and a kiss. "I love you."

"Love you too Dad," he said with a smile. Then he walked off with his equipment.

I was so moved by that scene. Who says that a father showing affection to his son is unmanly? That is the old world way of thinking. What I saw, was a strong, athletic young man who has confidence because he knows he is loved and supported.

I found it quite a co-incidence to have witnessed this just as I was finishing off this book. But being a man of God, I don't really believe in co-incidences. This was definitely a sign, and really re-enforced for me the reason I wrote this book.

Although he is no longer with us, I want to thank Anthony Viscardi for being such an inspiration to me. He was part of the many reasons I chose to write this book.

Just to let you know Anth', your boys are doing good.

I have to offer special thanks to my wife. She has made me realize that I had to forgive myself first, before I could forgive my father. Joanne went through a hell of her own with her ex, and with coming to terms with her childhood and letting go of anger. Without her, I don't think anyone else could have split my hard head, and got me to realize what I can and can't expect. It's like the St. Francis prayer:

*God grant me the serenity to accept the things I cannot change,*
*The strength to change the things I can*
*And the wisdom to know the difference*

In the end the only thing we can truly change is ourselves. Healing comes from within before it goes out, and hopefully we can touch others by our example. If we don't, then at least it won't bother us. I can't say that I am totally there yet. I am still working on it, and some days I have bad days where the depression about what could have been gets to me, but those days are becoming fewer.

I've started a daily ritual in our home that I believe will keep us close as a family and build the kids' self-esteem. I want them to always remember how much they are loved, not just by me, but by their mom and siblings too. I shout out:

"Group hug!"

Everyone comes running for the daily family hug. My kids at five and seven love this. Sometimes we get busy and Abigail will remind me:

"Daddy! Group hug!"

Something like this changes the mood for the whole day. If I come home from a crappy day at work, this really cheers me up, also no matter how cranky my son is, he will always answer the group hug call and be more cheerful afterward.

When my kids are older and able to read this, I want them to know that their nonno was always good to them. I don't want them to judge him by the way he was to me.

My father is still with us. He had a battle with colon cancer in which he was very lucky to survive. Seeing him lying in that hospital bed made me realize how much I did love him, flawed as he is. If nothing else he is my father! My reason for being alive! Whatever he may have done to me, things weren't always so bad. I had a home, I had food on the table, and I have happy childhood memories. These are the things I need to hold on to.

Peace of Christ be with you!

Made in the USA
Middletown, DE
31 March 2017